hip
hoptionary

the dictionary of hip hop terminology

ALONZO WESTBROOK

harlem moon
broadway books
new york

HIP HOPTIONARY.™ Copyright © 2002 by Alonzo Westbrook. All rights reserved. No part of this book may be reproduced or transmitted in any form or by any means, electronic or mechanical, including photocopying, recording, or by any information storage and retrieval system, without written permission from the publisher. For information, address Broadway Books, a division of Random House, Inc., 1540 Broadway, New York, NY 10036.

Harlem Moon titles may be purchased for business or promotional use or for special sales. For information, please write to: Special Markets Department, Random House, Inc., 280 Park Avenue, New York, NY 10017.

PRINTED IN THE UNITED STATES OF AMERICA

The figure in the Harlem Moon logo is inspired by a graphic design by Aaron Douglas (1899–1979). Harlem Moon and its logo, depicting a moon and woman, are trademarks of Broadway Books, a division of Random House, Inc.

Visit our website at www.harlemmoon.com

First edition published November 2002.

Designed by Elizabeth Rendfleisch

Cataloging-in-publication data is on file with the Library of Congress

ISBN 0-7679-0924-0

10 9 8 7 6 5 4

. . . Many thanks,

To the day-by-day ruler for being wonderfully mysterious. I never know what's going to happen next. I look forward to next time.

To mom for questioning my intent and for thoroughly assisting me once she knew I meant business.

To pop for keeping close tabs to make sure I was all right during those late nights of typing and research.

To bruhvie and sissie for the dough, thanks for coming thru.

To my friends for staying in touch, keeping it real, and helping me think beyond my own little space of mind.

To Illy for designing the illest book cover on the first edition. It is now a collector's item.

To E. Lynn Harris, for the mention. Thanks, bruh for the hookup.

To my Doubleday cohorts, Mark Hurst and Debbie Cowell, for adding the "mumbo sauce" to make this book sizzle! You're a terrific copy editor and editor, respectively.

Finally, to Janet Hill a.k.a. "J-Hi," who, from high up in her midtown Manhattan office, manages to keep an ear to the street. Thanks for finding me. You da' bomb, fa'sho!

Peace and blessings.
Zoe

Twenty years ago, naysayers said rap would die. Instead, it has exploded. Its words give it meaning.

Its creators give it life.

Caveat: There is no way I alone can know everything about hip-hop given the output the creative forces allow, but this is an attempt. The purpose of the book is to capture the language and preserve the culture of hip-hop, and also for the book to be used as a tool for education. This book is a living document, which simply put, means it is ever-changing. This is part two in a series. Read, laugh, but especially, enjoy.

It is only in his music, which Americans are able to admire because a protective sentimentality limits their understanding of it, that the Negro has been able to tell his story.

—james baldwin

acknowledgments

When the choice was life or death, you gave me reason to live.
To Ky, Steven, and Myka

ACE, Adrienne T. Washington, the *Washington Times*; Angel, Anjee, April (Earl's girl), "Big bang" Joshua, Bob Meadows, Bobcat, Carla Lawson, Charles A. Pugh, Charles, Earl, John, Gram, Chris Williams aka C-Poetic, Chuck and Mel at Nu Graphix, Damon, Darren Vaughn bka Self-D, David McGee aka D Mack/Mack G, Dean, Amelia, Brit and Bill, Dee Dee Hutson, Deena and Jade, Ellen Valentine, Falesha, Pat, Eileen and Roz at Natural Effects Hair Salon in Jacksonville, FL; Felicia, Z and Mario at Jambolayah; Donald "Friend" Tibbs, Gerald Smith and Ken Coleman WQBH Back-to-Back, Gregory Waterman, Hussani Phillip Drake II and III, Illy the artist, James Wilson at the U.S. Trademark Office, Joe L. Gleaton, Jr., The *CBS Early Show* crew Julie, Bryant, Carol and Debbie for the national exposure, John Spaulding, M.D., my boy Julius Kline, Kahn Davidson, the *Michigan Citizen*; Kevin Powell, Kimber "Boonk" Settles-Bryant, Kristi C. Harris, Kyra (Earl's daughter), L'Amour Larry Savoy at the U.S. Copyright Office, Lee Murray, Lou at the FBI, Lorena Craighead, Matteo Marcello Vocino for the pics, Margot at the United States Information Agency for the international exposure, Michael Greene, Michael Johnson, Ms. J. at Ethnic E'legance' in Jacksonville, FL, Nkenge Abi at The Shrine of the Black Madonna, Norris Schell, Quentin "Mistic" Hershey, cousin Quincy, Regina and Octavia, Sara Bruya aka Sweetsarab, Sankofa at Black Star Community Books, Steven Moses, T. L. Link, The Little Professor Book Center in Dearborn, Tom Pope-Mr. Powernomics, Toni Hickey, Ms. Vanessa "V" Howard, Vanessa Tyler, Victor Matthews, Zana at Spectacles, Lee White—the bodyguard.

Rap is like a slave song speaking of the conditions and hopes of a people, spinning words and communicating ideas in codes; hiding behind a language only to reveal its absolute strength and metaphorical depths.

The subversion of the language is the art form. But it is nothing new. Consider Muhammad Ali "floating like a butterfly and stinging like a bee" in the '70s, the Jive-talk of the '20s, or back farther when recently transported Africans were forced to code the language as a direct means of survival because by law slaves were not permitted to read or write.

In the language of rap, like the "languages" of the past, is the spontaneous expression of words. Artists write what they feel. They speak what they live and know and sometimes must. There is humor, deceit, and anguish that exposes and glamorizes urban madness, that turns the real and ugly into poetry, while resonating an emotional intensity that is matched by only the best in literary affairs.

With natural storytelling ability, rappers offer challenges, if you will, subtle and overt, angry and academic, playful and political in an effort it would seem, to get those who can make a difference to understand and to move beyond understanding to evolution.

Through catchy tunes, inventive phrases, and expressive voices rappers address the concerns and hopes of America in ways "intellectuals" have not or cannot because they are removed from "this" society. In doing so, they communicate history—they collect it, speak it and keep it alive. And despite what critics may say, by all indications, this music, these words are doing more good than harm. Any rapper will tell you, if he or she wasn't doing the rap hustle, they would be doing a street hustle. The only possible harm, then, is that rap exposes sides of the conscience, like sexism, racism, and poverty that mainstream does not want to hear, but needs to hear. Perhaps this is why the art has been betrayed and stereotypified by critics intent on collective judgment who have overlooked the significance of the movement with its artistry, lyrics, and poetry.

It is art. You have to work to get it and that requires a certain amount of sophistication. It's worldy and world changing art. It is peaceful art.

Who would have thought especially in these tims of hate and terror, that the brash and brazen hip-hop artists' choice for words and word combinations would be words of peace? Yet through their words historic barriers between races have fallen, allowing at once, strangers and enemies to vibe in concert; global friendships are being formed, the essence of which no words can truly define.

The flowering of Negro expression continues . . .

welcome to a new world of words

a: going to do something. "I'm *a* get me one of them when I make it big."

a-1: excellent.

Aaliyah: Aaliyah Haughton (1979–2001), female hip-hop artist. Detroit native. Aaliyah died in a plane crash at age twenty-two after filming a music video in the Bahamas.

A&R: initials stand for "artist and repertoire." A record company executive who finds new talent for his company and takes care of the needs of the talent within the company.

abc-ya: a way of saying good-bye.

above the rim: the highest level (derived from basketball, and a strong player's ability to jump extremely high in order to make an authoritative dunk).

Ac': Acura vehicle.

ace-boon-koon: friend.

ace-deuce: best friend.

acey-deucey: bisexual.

acquire: steal.

act a donkey: behave wildly.

act like you know: a threat or warning to not challenge the unknown.

addy: address. "What's ya *addy*, yo?"

aerosol artists: graffiti artists.

Afrika Bambaataa: Lance Aasim, DJ on the forefront of extending the scope of hip-hop. Bambaataa expanded hip-hop by mixing different types of national and international music. Credited with creating the Zulu Nation, a peaceful organization of musicians opposed to gang violence.

afro humanistic: 1) being true to one's African American spirit. 2) having respect for the African American culture and its people.

a-g: aggravated; upset.

aggie: angry.

aiight/ah-ight: all right, everything is okay.

ain't: is not.

ain't no shame in my game: statement of confidence while doing what could be perceived as a shameful act, i.e., having sex with a married man.

air tracks: a type of break dance.

ajax: clean, like the name-brand cleaning product.

AKs: military assault rifle, often referred to in rap lyrics.

a.k.a.: always known as/also known as.

a-level artist: top-selling artist.

Alize: alcoholic beverage.

all gravy: good.

all hell broke loose: bad things started to happen.

all net: perfect basketball shot.

all over it: in control of a situation.

all that: stellar, as good as it gets.

alla': all of.

Alpine: brand of car speakers.

alterna-rap: movement on the outskirts of rap that attempts to return rap to lyrics of substance.

amped: excited, raised level of activity.

angel dust: PCP.

Anomalies: all-female antimisogynist female hip-hop collective.

anyhoo: whatever, anyhow.

ape: animalistic. "He went *ape* when he found out he didn't get the contract."

architects: the originators of hip-hop or those who develop a new style within the hip-hop culture.

are you ready to throw down?: a call-and-response party chant. The response: "Yes, we are," spoken to the beat of music.

around the way: from the neighborhood.

around the way girl: clean, wholesome, respectable girl/woman.

around the world: full-service sex.

art crime: graffiti.

ASCAP, ESAC, BMI: agents who collect fees to make sure artists get paid for play of their licensed music.

ass out: 1) asleep. 2) out of luck/chances. 3) act out or misbehave. "We were all here trying to have a good time, but he had to *ass out* and mess things up for everybody."

assed out: 1) caught out there. 2) played.

A-State: Arkansas.

at: to. "Let me holla *at* you for a second."

ate out: 1) saggy look in the pants where the butt isn't visible—the pants are usually too big or dirty and worn. "He's looking *ate out* in those jeans." 2) oral sex on a female.

A-T-L/A-Town: Atlanta, Georgia.

ATLiens: residents of Atlanta, Georgia.

A Tribe Called Quest: Bohemian hip-hop group famous for funk grooves, jazzy rhythms, and intelligent lyrics. Members included Phife (Malik Taylor), Shaheed (Ali Muhammad), and Q-Tip (Kamaal Fareed a.k.a. Jonathan Davis). A.k.a. ATCQ.

attitude: disposition, negative or positive, to reflect one's mood. "She thought she was the best dressed at the party and was giving major *attitude*."

A.U.C.: Atlanta University Center. Group of Black colleges located in Southwest Atlanta, Georgia. They include Morehouse, Spelman, Clark-Atlanta University, Morris Brown, Morehouse School of Medicine, and Morehouse Theological Seminary.

Audi: to leave, be out. "I'm *Audi*."

aural candy: pleasing to the ear.

ave.: avenue.

ayo': A greeting meaning "a, you" or "hello, you."

azz: ass, as in butt.

b <<<

b: term of familiar address. "What's up, *b*?"

babe/baby: 1) term of endearment. 2) anything desirable. "I'm a get me one of them *babies* when I get paid Friday."

baby boy: a term of familiar address, usually to young males.

baby daddy: the father of a woman's child when the parents are not married.

baby got back: girl with a big butt.

baby momma: the mother of a man's child when the parents are not married.

Baby Phat: clothing label created by Def Jam record executive Russell Simmons and his wife, Kimora Lee. The line features women's apparel. It's a spin-off of Simmons's Phat Farm clothing label.

bacdafucup: "back the fuck up," meaning "stop making a commotion" or "step back."

back: butt.

back dat ass up: "back that ass up," "come here." A request, usually to a stripper, to return to a customer she walked away from.

back in the day: refers to a time past, usually a good memory.

back packer: a style, usually the look of oversized clothing, hoodies, and a backpack.

back spinning: DJ technique using two turntables. DJ plays one record while turning the record on a second turntable backward, repeating phrases and beats in a rhythmic manner (see **Grandmaster Flash**).

backslide: a break dance. The dance was mislabeled the moonwalk. "Michael Jackson made the *backslide* dance popular."

backyard boogy: bad (not good) marijuana.

bacon: police.

bad: means good. "That dress she's wearing is *bad*."

bag/bag (ged) up: 1) jailed. 2) reference to a dead person. "He got *bagged* last night in a drive by." 3) killed. 4) sexed.

bale: really good. The bomb. (Cape Verde)

ball: 1) to have a good time. "We had a *ball*." 2) cry. "She *balled* all night long over that man." 3) to sex. "Did you *ball* her?" 4) world. 5) basketball. 6) universe.

ball out: have a good time.

baller: 1) professional sports player. 2) lavish spender. 3) drug dealer.

baller blocker: someone who stands in the way of success.

balls: 1) bravado. 2) testicles.

bama: 1) short for Alabama, the state. 2) backward, unsophisticated (in this sense, *bama* can be considered offensive).

bamboozled: tricked (attributed to Malcolm X).

bananas: 1) crazy. 2) off the hook. 3) good.

bang: jail.

banger: 1) good song. 2) fighter (see **gang-banger**).

bangin': 1) selling drugs. 2) having sex. 3) fighting. 4) anything pleasing.

bangin' boots/knocking boots: having sex.

bank (roll): a bunch of money, usually rolled and in a money clip.

bankhead bounce: a dance best described by jackhammer head movements and jerking shoulder gyrations. The name comes from a highway in Atlanta, Georgia. (GA)

bar: musical measurement. One bar equals four counts. It's counted one, two, three, four, repeat to the beat of a song. The bar count is used to measure how long an emcee will rap in an emcee battle. It could be 8, 16, 32 bars, or more.

bar up: buy a drink at a bar.

bashment: a party (Jamaica).

bass beats: sounds simulated on a drum machine or created by a bass guitar.

battle/me battle: war between or among rappers, dancers, DJs, or emcees for prizes or bragging rights and to see who is the best. Winner is judged by crowd applause on originality. When lyrics are involved it's what's said and how it is delivered—the cadence and complexity of the lyrics; if music is used, the originality and quality of production also are judged.

battle board: online site where emcees stage lyrical battles.

Bay: San Francisco, California.

b-ball: basketball.

b-boy: break-boy. A break-dancer, originally, one who danced during the break of a song. The "break" is when the singer stops for a break and the instrumental part begins.

BDS: Broadcast Data System—a company that tracks radio play.

B.E.T.: Black Entertainment Television, a channel on the cable network that caters to a Black audience and features news and views of Black America.

bezzled out: the dazzle in watch, jewelry; compare **bling bling.** (AL)

be out: leave.

beam me up, Scotty: request for crack cocaine.

beamed: cleaned up.

Beamer/BM: BMW, European car.

beans: little money; pocket change. "He counting *beans* until payday."

Beantown: Boston, Massachusetts.

beat: 1) well dressed or well groomed. "She was *beat* in that Versace outfit." 2) fake.

beat-down: 1) to beat up severely. "Money took a serious *beat-down* for dropping dime." 2) well dressed or groomed.

Beatdown: rap's first newspaper.

beating cakes: having sex.

beat jackers: music thieves.

beat junkies: lovers of the freewheeling hip-hop music.

beat-maker: music producer.

beat master: master DJ.

beat-mining: the process of creating new music.

beats: music.

beat the rap: 1) to be acquitted. 2) to have charges dropped.

Bed-Stuy: Bedford-Stuyvesant. Neighborhood in Brooklyn, New York.

beef: 1) to have a problem with. 2) penis.

beeper codes:
    1–2—as in one-two punch. It means "call me."
    5–0—police. "Watch out."
    10–4—okay.
    50–50—undecided.
    86—"I'm gone" or "I'm leaving."
    143—"I love you" (number of letters per word).
    711—it's a winning dice combination. It means "Want to get lucky?"
    1040—(IRS form) "Where is my money?"
    1812—(War of 1812) fight, beef.
    411—the latest scoop or information.
    504—a New Orleans area code.
    7734–02–09—(read upside down) "Go to hell."

beeswax: 1) business. "What he do with her is none of your *beeswax.*" 2) hair solution used on dreadlocks.

bee-yotch: "bitch" with playful stresses on the word (also see **bitch**).

b-girl: break-girl. A break-dancer, originally, one who danced during the break of a song. The "break" is when the singer stops for a break and the instrumental part begins.

be-geesee: be gone/to leave.

behind God's back: in the middle of nowhere. "The reason it took us so long to get to her house is because she lives out there *behind God's back.*"

behind the wall: in jail.

belly/belly of the beast: 1) jail. 2) difficult situation.

Belvi: Belvedere vodka.

bend: 1) a term used to describe a female in a sexual sense. 2) sex act. 3) prostitute.

Benjamins: hundred-dollar bills. Called *Benjamins* because Benjamin Franklin's face is on the bill.

bent: drunk.

Bentley: handmade car.

be out: leave, or go. "I'm 'bout to *be out*," or "You need to *be out* now."

berry: police officer.

bested: won.

bet: agree. "That's a *bet*."

Betty: attractive female. (Derived from *The Flintstones*—Wilma was aiight, but Betty was really the fly one.)

Bettys: pretty girls.

bg: 1) baby gangster. Someone new to crime. 2) (see **b-girl**).

bia bia: bitch.

bid: jail time.

big bodies: SUVs or luxury vehicles.

Big Daddy: 1) big spender. 2) man with power.

big dog/dawg: 1) the person in charge. 2) the person who has gained/ earned/demanded respect.

Big Easy: New Orleans, Louisiana.

big face money: large bills.

big fatty: cigar dumped of its tobacco and filled with marijuana.

big head: swollen ego.

big macs: big breasts.

big numbers: prison term.

Big Pun/Big Punisher: Christopher Rios. First Latino rapper to sell one million records (platinum). Passed away February 7, 2000, of a heart attack.

big time(r): 1) one who lives extravagantly. 2) large amount/capacity. "She ripped him off *big time*."

big-ups: 1) boost sound. 2) respect. "I give him *big-ups* for doing that record so well."

Big Willie: 1) flashy, extravagant male. 2) a Will Smith moniker.

Big Willona: the female version of "Big Willie"—flashy, extravagant female.

Biggie: (See **Notorious B.I.G**).

biggin' up: 1) boasting. 2) complimenting.

Billboard: a magazine that, among other things, compiles lists of record sales in all genres.

bing: jail.

bird: 1) key of cocaine. 2) female. 3) person who is in and out of jail; also, jailbird.

biscuit: pretty girl.

biscuit head: ugly girl.

bit: AIDS.

bitch: 1) strong, confident, secure woman. 2) person with a nasty, negative disposition. 3) soft, passive person.

bitch-ass-niggas: passive or fearful person(s).

bitchin': 1) complaining. 2) pleasing to the senses.

bite/bitin'/biter: copycat.

biz: business. "I'm about the *biz*, I'm not concerned with anything else."

biz-zank: bank a.k.a. money (see **izzo language**).

bizzo: girl.

BK: 1) Brooklyn, New York. 2) Burger King restaurant.

b.k.a.: better known as.

Black Lily: female-centric weekly performance outlet in NYC and Philly.

blacktop: city street.

blah-blah: blabber.

Blak/blacc: black and mild cigars.

blasé-blah: borderline boring. "The party was *blasé-blah*."

blast shots: fire a weapon.

Blatino: person of Black and Latino descent.

blaze: 1) sex. 2) marijuana. 3) to wear. 4) defunct hip-hop magazine.

blazin': 1) smoking weed. 2) having sex. 3) anything pleasing to the senses.

blazing the charts: rising in the ranks on the hip-hop music charts.

bless the mic: offer great rap.

blick: bad situation.

blicky: 1) AIDS. "He has the *blickey*." 2) gun.

bling bling: 1) jewelry. 2) material showoff. 3) the glitter of diamonds.

blinked out: went crazy.

blip music: original game music that complements a video and its action.

blood: 1) term of familiar address. 2) brother. (MW)

Bloods: L.A. street gang.

blow: 1) ruin, as in "ruin a chance." 2) cocaine.

blower: telephone.

blowin' in the wind: lost.

blowin' smoke: talking trash.

blowin' trees: smoking marijuana.

blowin' up: 1) excelling; gaining in popularity. 2) constantly calling someone on the telephone. "She be *blowin up* my phone, so I'm turning it off."

blow job: oral sex performed on a man.

blow off: show no interest.

blow-out: 1) a large Afro 2) sex party with more than two people. (TN) 3) sold-out event. 4) flat tire.

blow up the spot: give an outstanding performance.

blow up your/his/her/my spot: to embarrass in front of a group of people "We were all just hanging out talking and his moms came and *blew up his spot*."

blown up: to have achieved success.

blueballs: male sexual frustration.

blunt: marijuana rolled in cigar paper.

BMX: bicycle.

boards: 1) music producers' mixing board. 2) keyboards.

boat: 1) marijuana mixed with embalming fluid. 2) New York subway.

bob: marijuana cigarette.

bodega: 1) convenience store. 2) weed house. 3) party spot.

bodied: 1) slammed body-to-body. 2) fought. 3) killed.

body rock: break dancing.

body rockers: break dancers.

bogard: 1) stingy. 2) hoard. 3) push through. "He tried to *bogard* his way into the club."

bogies: marijuana cigarettes.

boilers: cars.

bold: 1) brave. 2) bad. "That was some *bold* shit she did fuckin' his boy."

bomb: 1) good. "That song is the *bomb*." 2) marijuana mixed with heroin. 3) fail. 4) to write on (graffiti).

bombay: good.

bombin' the streets: writing (graffiti).

bone yard: cemetery.

bone: 1) have sex. 2) a marijuana cigarette. 3) regular cigarette. "Let me get a *bone* and a light?" 4) penis.

bones: 1) dollars. 2) dominos.

bonkers: good.

boo: 1) girlfriend or boyfriend. 2) term of endearment.

boob tube: television.

boo-boo the fool: foolish person.

boobs: breasts.

boodah: marijuana

boogee: bourgeois.

Boogie/Boogie Down: Bronx, New York. The New York City borough where hip-hop began in the '70s. A.k.a. BX.

book of words: dictionary.

book: 1) flee. 2) schedule.

books: account.

boom boom room: playroom for adults.

boom box: radio.

boom-bap: fusion of jazz and hip-hop.

boomin': 1) loud. 2) good sounding. "That bass is *boomin'*." 3) prospering.

boondocks (also boonies): the middle of nowhere. "No one comes to visit you because you live in the *boondocks*."

boost/boof: steal.

boot up: prepare.

boot: kick out or get rid of.

bootleg: stolen merchandise sold on the streets.

bootsy: 1) bad, not good. 2) crazy. (CA)

booty/booty call: wee-hour-in-the-morning phone call after everything is closed and the party is over to arrange a sexual encounter.

booty club: strip club.

booty music/tracks: hard bass music, usually with explicit lyrics.

bootylicious: sexy.

boo-yaa: an exclamation to something good.

Boricua, Morena: person of mixed Black and Hispanic heritage. *Boricua* means Puerto Rican. *Morena* means dark.

boss/bossman: 1) term of familiar address, mostly used to address an up-wardly mobile person. 2) white man. 3) authority figure.

boughetto: combination of the terms *bourgeois* and *ghetto*. (MO)

bounce music: Southern-style music with heavy bass beat and hypnotic chants.

bounce: 1) to leave. 2) to cruise in a car. 3) to be thrown out, dismissed. "They *bounced* him right out of the club. 4) fight. 5) a dance (see **bankhead bounce**). 6) visit.

bout it, bout it: in support of, willing.

box: vagina.

boys in blue: police.

brainfood: useful information.

brand new: newly adopted attitude because of recent good fortune or success.

Brass Monkey: alcoholic beverage.

break: the part in an old school song where the singer would pause for an instrumental part. During the *break*, deejays would rap and b-boys would *break* dance.

break beat DJ: DJ who also acts as emcee. He/she recites rhymes during the break in a record. When the singer pauses for a break and the instruments kick in, the deejay does his emcee thing.

break camp: leave.

break dancing: freestyle dancing, usually with fast movements, flips, and spins. Originally, the dance was done during the break of a song when a singer takes a break and the instrumental part kicks in, hence, break dance. Some of the dances include pop locking, electric boogaloo, and backsliding (moonwalk).

break it down: explain.

break off: give money, share.

break out: leave. "I'm about to *break out* of here, so I'll holla later."

breaks: bad luck. "These are the *breaks*."

brew/brewski: beer.

brick: 1) cold weather. 2) large quantity. 3) hundred-dollar bill. 4) drugs. 5) records.

Brick City/The Bricks: Newark, New Jersey.

bricked: failed.

bring it: deliver.

bro/bruh: 1) term of familiar address. 2) brother.

broke: 1) out of money. 2) fled.

brown showers: shit, poo-poo. To literally shit on somebody or to be shit on.

brown sugah/sugar: pretty black girl.

b.s.: bullshit.

B-Town: Berkeley, California.

bubblegum rap: similar-sounding electronic-driven music you can put any voice to and make the song work.

bubblin': exciting. "Keep it *bubblin'*."

bubbly: giddy.

buck: 1) intimidate. 2) sex. 3) kill.

buck the system: to get what you need in ways not in accordance with the system.

buck wild: acting without restraint or concern for the consequences. "The DJ showed up late to the party and everyone just went *buck wild*, so they had to shut the club down."

bucket: raggedy car.

bud: marijuana.

buddah: marijuana.

buddah lips: lips that have turned dark from smoking too much weed.

bug-a-boo: loser.

buggin'/buggin' out: 1) to act weird. 2) to dance well.

bullshit: bad, not good.

bump: 1) a dance. It's simply bumping hips to the beat of music. 2) have sex. 3) anything that looks and sounds good. "That new song by Erykah Badu is *bumpin'*." 4) kill.

bumping gums: talking.

bump-in-yo-trunk: 1) extra speakers in a car trunk to give added sound. 2) big butt.

bumpkin: 1) a Southern-acting or -sounding person. 2) backward, unsophisticated. 3) person from the Southern USA.

bumrush: 1) to hit or enter another person's space without warning. 2) fight. 3) ambush.

bunk: junk.

b-up: 1) stay cool. 2) positive reinforcement.

burb: suburb.

burn: 1) play a song on video or radio; airplay. "That video got a little *burn* but not much." 2) to give a venereal disease. 3) to set up for danger. 4) write (graffiti).

burner: 1) gun. 2) good record. 3) art (graffiti).

bush: pubic hair.

bust/bust this: 1) request to check something out. "*Bust this!*" 2) to wear. "I'm gone *bust this* at the party tomorrow." 3) to physically hit. "I'm a *bust* that dude in the mouth he keep talkin'." 4) to catch doing wrong. "You're *busted*." 5) to start. "*Bust* a move, dawg." 6) to leave. "I'm bout to *bust* up out of here."

busta/bustah: 1) person who spoils a good time. 2) snitch. 3) unfamiliar person. "Who is that *bustah*?" 4) wimp.

bust a cap: shoot a gun, fire a bullet. "If he doesn't shut up I'm a *bust a cap* in his behind."

bust a nut: ejaculate.

bust a rhyme: rap.

Busta Rhymes: Trevor Smith, rapper, actor. Flamboyant, colorful rapper known for his lyrical outbursts. Created Bushi hip-hop clothing line.

busted: 1) ugly, raggedy. 2) caught.

busted my balls: 1) worked hard. 2) chewed out for doing wrong.

bust me down: "Save me the second half of your cigarette" (usually only among close friends, "Yo' *bust me down*, son.").

busy: active in other folks' business.

busybody: active person.

busy-lips: 1) talkative person. 2) one who indulges in oral sex.

butch: male-acting lesbian.

butt: bad, not good. "That music is *butt*." "He's *butt* ugly."

buttah/butter: smooth.

Butta Pecan Rican: pretty Puerto Rican female.

buttas: leaders, creative thinkers in the world of hip-hop.

butter: money.

butterfly: a dance in which legs spread out like butterfly wings.

buzz: high on drugs.

bwoy: boy.

BX: Bronx, New York (see **Boogie Down**).

cabbage: 1) money. 2) a person's head.

cadi/caddy: Cadillac, luxury vehicle made by General Motors.

Caesar: low haircut

caged: 1) jailed. 2) mentally locked in.

cake: money.

cake mixing: 1) having sex. 2) talking on the phone, chit-chatting.

caked up: feeling the effects of drugs.

cali: 1) California. 2) marijuana.

called out: singled out.

camel jockeys: Arabs (offensive).

camp: 1) prison. 2) any other location, i.e., recording studio, someone else's house, restaurant. "I'm about to break this *camp* any minute now." 3) headquarters.

campaigning: selling. "I caught a case while down here *campaigning* in the dope game."

can: 1) toilet stall, bathroom. 2) to terminate.

cancer sticks: cigarettes.

candy: good.

candy bar: pretty girl.

candy man: drug dealer.

candy paint: paint job on a car.

can't hold a candle to me: doesn't compare.

cap: 1) bullet. "I'm a put a *cap* in his ass." 2) to shoot. 3) to tell a joke.

cap-cocked: the way a hat is worn tilted to the side.

caper: business.

cappers: bad rappers with simple rhymes.

carrying on: exhibiting rude or obnoxious behavior.

cased: checked out, searched. "We *cased* the joint once we got in."

casper: to leave, disappear, derived from the ghost.

cat(s): 1) term of familiar description. "That *cat* is new to town I've never seen him before."/"That's my *cat* I hang out with all the time." 2) vagina.

catch a case: 1) to get upset. 2) lawsuit.

catching bodies: lyrically killing an opponent in an emcee battle.

cat eye: look of seduction.

caveman: white male.

cavewoman: white female.

cb: 1) prison cellblock. 2) "cockblocking"—sexual interference.

CCE: "continuing criminal enterprise,"—criminal charge against someone believed to be shot caller of criminal operation resulting from information usually gathered from wire taps on the suspect.

cellar: underground or nonmainstream rap music.

cells: 1) brain; ability to think. "She ain't got no *cells*, dog." 2) the amount of charge on a cellular phone.

celly: cell phone.

cess: marijuana.

chale: no way! (NM)

chamber: 1) style. 2) chamber of a gun.

check my window: check the caller ID.

check(ed) out: 1) died. 2) an order to kill. "*Check* him *out* tomorrow night." 3) request to observe, consider, and possibly offer a response. 4) consider.

check yourself before you wreck yourself: consider actions.

cheddar: money.

cheeba: marijuana.

cheese: 1) money. 2) yeast buildup on unclean or uncircumcised males.

cheesin': hamming it up.

cherry: blood that presents itself after penetrating a virgin; to break the hymen of a virgin is to have gotten her *cherry*.

Cherry Mild: cherry-flavored cigar.

Chester: someone who has sex with someone much younger. "*Chester, Chester*, child molester."

chewin': oral sex. (TN)

chew stick: flavored stick people chew on but don't eat. They come in different flavors.

Chi/Chi-Town: Chicago, Illinois.

chi-chi: trendy.

chi-ching: money (sound from the ringing of a cash register).

chick: female.

chicken head: female who performs oral sex—head moves back and forth like a chicken; also used as an insult.

chill/chillin': relax/relaxing.

chill-out room: cozy room insight a nightclub that has seating for patrons to chitchat and relax under low-sounding music.

Chinx: Chinese people (offensive).

chips: money.

Chitlin Circuit: tour circuit for local and regional acts.

Chocolate City: Washington, District of Columbia (DC), the nation's capital.

choke: marijuana.

chop-chop: marijuana.

chop up: to make key words repeat in a song. (TX)

chopper: assault rifle, namely AK-47, named such because it dissembles or chops parts of the body away from the whole. (DS)

Chopper City: New Orleans, Louisiana.

chopping: talking.

chops: 1) teeth. 2) raps.

Chris Rock: comedian who uses his life in the ghetto as fodder for his jokes; as such, is called a hip-hop comedian.

chrome: gun.

chronic: marijuana.

chronic flakes: marijuana ashes.

Chucks/Chuck Taylor: Converse All-Stars, a brand of gym shoes.

ciddity: uppity; snobbish.

cipher/cipher: 1) life experiences. 2) event where artists go one at a time displaying/exhibiting their craft/talent in an unbroken circle. 3) conversation. 3) 360—the number of degrees in a full circle.

Cita: virtual reality character with video show on BET called *Cita's World*.

clash: contest for superiority among members of any of the groups in the four elements of hip-hop. Winner is determined by crowd applause (see **battle**).

clean rap: rap without profanity, violence, or misogyny.

Click-Click: name given to New Orleans, Louisiana, because of its high murder rate.

clock: 1) to hit, as in physically punch. 2) to see through pretense. 3) to earn. "He's *clocking* dollars." 4) to watch.

clock out: die.

clown: 1) to do well. 2) to argue. 3) to act silly. 4) to make a fool of.

clowning: 1) making people laugh. 2) exhibiting angry and offensive behavior. "He got drunk and started *clowning*."

club banger: good song.

club rat: one who parties all the time.

C-notes: hundred-dollar bills.

cockblock/CB: to create sexual interference. "Tell her to go home and stop *cockblocking*."

cocked: ready to throw a punch.

cock diesel: big and muscular.

coconut: white-acting Hispanic person.

coins: money.

cojones: bravado.

Coke bottles: thick eyeglasses.

cold: 1) good, nice. "That suit is *cold*." 2) mean. 3) sleep in the eyes from being tired.

collabo: collaboration.

collar poppin': feeling good; relaxing.

come at me, dog: challenge to fight or do battle in some other format, i.e., music, sports, etc.

comeback cat: person able to recover from a bad episode.

come correct: 1) to approach with respect. 2) to do correctly.

come for me: attack verbally or physically (see **come at me, dog**).

come hard: come with your best.

come to grips: accept and get over.

comp(s): company or companies.

concrete jungle: urban city streets.

confama: the combination of "confused" and "drama" to mean confused drama.

confiscate: steal.

constama: the combination of "constant" and "drama" to mean constant drama.

contact: high off the smell of marijuana.

coochie: vagina.

coochie-poppin-grooves: songs that make you want to dance. (see **rump shaker**).

coodagras: vagina.

cookies: butt.

cool: acceptable.

cool breeze: a mellow person.

Coolio: Artis Leon Ivey, Jr., rapper.

cool out: to relax, to be calm (see **chill/chillin'**).

co-opt: steal.

cop (ped): 1) to steal. **2)** to bargain for lesser charges offered in return for a confession or help in solving a police case. "He *copped* a plea so he wouldn't have to do a seven-year bid." **3)** to buy.

copastetic: good. (Webster's spells it *copacetic*.)

copyright: ownership of written lyrics or music of a song. Copyright office in Washington, DC 202.707.0612 or http://www.loc.gov/copyright.com

corn (y): nerd or nerdish-acting person.

Cornell West: renowned scholar and Harvard professor who calls hip-hop the greatest creative breakthrough of the last twenty-five years in his debut hip-hop CD, *Sketches of My Culture*.

cornerboy: male who hangs out all the time.

cornrows: braids. Southern legend attributes the name cornrows to a slavemaster who said the way the slaves braided their hair looked like rows of corn.

cos: companies.

co-sign: to back up.

country: 1) unsophisticated (offensive). **2)** Southern-acting or -sounding person.

county blues: prison-issued uniform.

cowboy: overzealous police officer.

C.P.T.: "Colored People Time," which generally is late.

CPT: Compton, California.

crab scratch: a deejaying technique where the DJ's fingers are twirled on a turntable simulating the movement of a crab.

crack: synthetic drug made from cocaine and baking soda.

cracker: white person (offensive).

crack head: crack addict.

crackin': happening; looking good, sounding good; making one feel good. "That song is *crackin'*."

crackin' up: laughing hard, almost uncontrollably.

crackitute: person who has sex in direct trade for crack cocaine.

crackulating: started. "Let's get *crackulating*."

crankin': anything pleasing. "That DJ was *crankin'*."

crazy: 1) unusual behavior but not necessarily certifiable by psychiatric standards. 2) fun/funny. "You so *crazy*."

C.R.E.A.M.: 1) "Cash Rules Everything Around Me," from the Wu Tang Clan. 2) money. (NY)

created a monster: by-product of someone's actions.

cred: credibility.

creep/creepin': 1) to sneak. 2) to have an adulterous affair.

Crescent City: New Orleans, Louisiana.

crew: tight-knit friends.

crib: place of dwelling.

Crips: L.A. street gang. A.k.a. Mainstreet Mafia, Mainstreet Crips, City Contact Crips. (CA)

Cris/Crissy: Cristal, an expensive champagne.

cronies: friends.

Cronkite: gossiper, person who tells other people's business, derived from the name of newsman Walter Cronkite.

Crooked-letter country: Mississippi.

Crooklyn: Brooklyn, New York.

crossing out: writing over someone else's graffiti.

crowd mover: 1) music that moves a crowd. 2) a person who hypes the crowd on a microphone (see **hype-man**).

crown: 1) head. 2) oral sex.

crunk/krunk: 1) crowded. 2) hyped. 3) exciting. 4) fun. (DS)

crying the blues: complaining; whining.

crystal methamphetamine: an illegal drug bought on the street, used as either an upper or downer. It's basically a hallucinogen. A.k.a. Tina.

C-Town: Cleveland, Ohio.

curtains: the beginning or end.

cut: 1) song on an album. 2) to leave. "I'm about to *cut*, I'll see y'all later." 3) home. "I'm heading to the *cut* after this session." 4) haircut. 5) to like/appreciate. "I *cut* for this magazine."

cut creator: 1) music producer. 2) video director.

cut his throat: a phrase use in lyrical competitions. To "cut his throat" is to silence a competitor by a stellar performance.

cut into: 1) to threaten with verbal or physical assault. 2) set straight on an issue. "I'm 'bout to *cut into* his ass if he don't give me my money."

cute: pretty face and alright body or vice versa, but not necessarily the whole package.

cutthroat: 1) highly competitive. 2) unforgiving.

cut (ting) up: 1) to act in an exaggerated manner for the sake of a good time. 2) to have a muscular body.

cuz/cuzzen: 1) term of familiar address. 2) cousin, blood relative.

c-ya (see you): "good-bye" or "see you later."

c-ya wouldn't want to be ya: statement made to one by another who feels he is better in terms of looks, employment, style, wealth, etc.

cyberskiing: to check soundscan. (see **soundscan**).

da: the. "Do *da* damn thang."

Da Brat: Shawntae Harris. Fun, hard-core rapper known for tomboyish attitude and cocky fast-paced rhymes. First female emcee to sell one million records (see **platinum**).

Daisy Dukes: cut-off shorts, derived from TV character and country girl Daisy Duke, who wore such shorts in the TV series *The Dukes of Hazzard*.

dank: 1) marijuana. 2) stylishly dressed.

dap: 1) a handshake. 2) to give credit for a creation.

dapper: well dressed, well groomed.

dark side: bad, not good.

darts: verbal insults thrown by rappers during competition. "We's throwing some serious *darts* in them."

dat: that.

dawg/dog: 1) to treat badly. "He *dogged* her." 2) term of familiar address. "Where my *dawgs* at?" 3) mean person.

day-by-day ruler: God.

dead: 1) end the discussion. 2) full.

dead on the money: exact.

Dead Presidents: money.

Deejay/DJ/Disc jockey: person who plays records to keep a party going and people on a dance floor.

deep: 1) profound statement or thought. 2) large amount. 3) depth of woman's vagina.

deep pockets: lots of money.

deeze: these.

def: good.

Def Comedy Jams: comedy showcase created by Russell Simmons.

delo: 1) the deal, or happening. "What's the *delo*?" 2) see **down lo/delo/the DL.**

De La Soul: rap trio who set the standard for socially conscious rap and consistently quality music. Maseo (Vincent Mason), Trugoy the Dove now known as Dave (Dave Jolicoeur), Posdnous (Kelvin Mercer). FYI: Trugoy is "yogurt" spelled backward.

demo: demonstration of artists' work.

Deuce O's: 20-inch rims.

diamond: term given to an album that has sold ten million copies.

Diane Martell: hip-hop video director.

dibs/dibbies: to stake claim on something. "I got *dibs* on the front seat."

dibby's down: refusal to a claim made on something.

dick: 1) mean person. 2) horseplay. 3) penis.

diesel: 1) hard, chiseled body, usually from exercising. 2) masculine, strong.

diesel dyke: female who dresses and acts like a male.

dig: 1) covert insult. "He took a *dig* at her outfit." 2) to understand. 3) to like. "I'm *diggin'* her."

diggin' for gold: digging in your nose with your fingers.

Digital Hip-Hop: producers of urban-themed animated videos for the Web.

digits: 1) phone number. "Did you get the *digits*?" 2) money.

digs: living quarters.

drop dime: 1) to tell. 2) $10 bag of marijuana. 3) pretty girl ("dime" equals 10 on the pretty woman rating scale).

dime: 1) pretty girl, a 10, à la Bo Derek. 2) $10 bag of marijuana. 3) to tell.

dip: 1) to invite oneself into another's conversation. "Quit dippin." 2) to leave. 3) short for honey dip.

dipped: well dressed.

dips: pickpockets.

dirty: 1) illegal. 2) see **Dirty South**. 3) cocaine.

dirty dozens: playful insults that attack a person's dignity.

Dirty South/DS: music map term for the Southern regions of the United States, roughly from Texas to New Orleans and the Gulf Coast to Georgia.

dis/dissin': to disrespect.

distression: state of distress.

ditty: thing.

diva: 1) pretty girl. 2) bitchy girl. 3) songstress.

dizzles: large lips.

DJ Jubilee: legendary bounce music DJ. A.k.a. King of Bounce Music.

DMX: Dark Man X. Earl Simmons. Rapper, actor. Famed for gangster rhymes, dog barking, and praying in song.

DNA: drugs and alcohol.

do: 1) hairdo. 2) to have sex with. "I'm gone *do* him."

doc: a term of familiar address. "What's up, *doc*?"

do-do: whack. "The music up in this club is *do-do*."

doe/dough: money.

dog food: bad, not good, raps/rhyme.

dogs/dawgs: 1) hanging crew, boys. 2) feet.

doin' dirt: acting immorally, illegally, or unethically.

doin' it well: 1) performing well, living well, etc. 2) experiencing top sexual performance.

dolo: self/solo.

dome: head, more specifically, the mind.

do me a solid?: do me a favor?

Don: 1) leader. 2) cool guy.

Don P: Dom Pérignon champagne.

Donald Goines: prolific author of ghetto life stories, 1938–74.

Dondadda chick: high-maintenance girl. "She one of them *Dondadda chicks.*"

done: 1) surprised, when outdone. 2) end. 3) beat up. 4) made up cosmetically.

done up: dressed up.

don't believe the hype: don't believe the rumors.

don't even try it: don't do it, don't think about doing it.

don't forget yourself: don't do something I asked you not to do.

don't get beside yourself: a warning to a smart-mouthed person: don't attempt to disrespect me.

don't get it twisted: don't mess up the facts.

don't go there: warning to leave subject alone.

don't play yourself: don't get your feelings hurt; don't do something obviously stupid to cause yourself to be embarrassed.

don't sleep: don't miss out.

donut shop: drug transaction center.

doobie: marijuana cigarette.

dookey ropes: thick gold rope chains.

dope: 1) drugs. 2) nice. 3) good.

do-rag: head rag used to keep hair in place.

do-right spirit: godly spirit.

double-deuce: .22-caliber pistol.

double fisted: two drinks, one in each hand.

Double H nation: hip-hop nation.

Double "R" nation: Ruff Ryders music label.

Doug E. Fresh: Rapper. Innovator of the human beat box—the ability to make beats using the mouth.

dough: money.

doves: females.

down: 1) included. "He's *down* with us." 2) up-to-date, current. 3) in agreement with. 4) to recommend. "I put him *down* with the boss, so he should get the job." 5) desire to be accepted. 6) to perform oral sex. "She went *down* on him in the bathroom at the church." 7) jail.

down by law: automatically included. "By law" is the nature of things.

down for the count: countdown, usually to a bad occurrence.

down lo/delo/the DL: discreet, low-key.

downtown: between a woman's legs.

do you: do your thing. "*Do you*, nigga." Don't worry about what other people think.

dozens: playful insults.

dragon: penis.

drama: exaggerated behavior or an overreaction to a situation that makes things worse.

drama's moma: heightened level of drama.

draw down: to smoke, inhale.

drawers: underwear.

Dr. Dre: Andre Young. Premier rapper, producer. Helped create funky, synthesized West Coast sound. Credited with taking the West Coast gangsta sound mainstream. Patterned name after Dr. J, the famous basketball great.

dreadlocks: 1) a hairstyle worn primarily by and associated with Rastafarian spirituality. The basis for dreadlocks comes from Numbers 6:5 in the Holy Bible: ". . . shall no razor come upon his head: until the days be fulfilled . . . (he) shall let the locks of the hair of his head grow." Non-Rastafarians also wear dreadlocks for various reasons. 2) hip-hop comic book by Andre L. Batts.

driveby: 1) shooting a gun while driving by someone's home. 2) to check out a scene. "We did a *driveby* of the club and there were no cars in the lot."

dro: marijuana (see **hydro**). (CA)

drop: 1) to kill. 2) to release a record.

drop dime: to tell on someone, derived from a person who dropped a dime in the phone to call the police, back when a call only cost a dime.

droppin' dime: snitching.

drops: promotional advertisement by an artist for upcoming album or for a radio station.

drop science: to teach.

drop science like an epileptic chemist: to teach a really serious lesson.

drop squad: collection of artists within a company.

drop-top: convertible vehicle.

drop track: record sound.

D's: 1) Dayton's, car rims. 2) detectives. (SC)

DSL's: dick-sucking lips.

dub: record of the original.

dub deuces: 22-inch rims.

dubs: car rims.

duck/duckettes/ducats: money.

ducks in a row: things in order.

duke: 1) term of familiar address. 2) fight.

dummin' up: not remembering, pretending to be forgetful.

dun: term of familiar address, like "man."

dust: cocaine.

dust blunt: marijuana laced with angel dust.

dusting: snorting drugs.

Dusty South: Oklahoma.

Dutch: 1) Dutch Masters cigars. 2) date where each pays his and her own expenses.

dyed, fried, and laid to the side: processed hair.

<<<

e/x/ex/love drug: the drug ecstasy.

ear-catching beats: beats that grab attention.

eargasmic/ear candy: pleasing sound.

earl: vomit.

ear to the ground: 1) keeping an ear out. 2) listening for new talent, scouting.

East Coast hip-hop: kill or be killed lyrics perhaps born out of the lawlessness spawned from rampant crack cocaine use and desperate living in oppressed conditions.

eats: food, restaurant.

eat that nigga: competitive language used during emcee battles. "Eat him up" means beat him in competition.

Eazy-E: Eric Wright. Rapper. Influential in establishing West Coast gangster-style music. Formed the rap group NWA. Founded Ruthless Records. Died of AIDS in 1995.

e-box: coffin.

EC: East Coast.

edutainer: rapper who entertains as well as educates through lyrics (see **KRS One**).

effin'/effin' up: fuckin' up. Term used instead of the four-letter "F" word. It means to ruin something.

E-40: Earl Stevens, rapper. West Coast rapper famous for his unpredictable rap style and use of slanguage.

ego-trippin: overly boastful.

e-i: A saying made famous by rapper Nelly. It's more or less an exclamatory saying. (MO)

eight ball: eight-ounce bag of cocaine, usually the measurement bought to make crack from.

89th key: the voice. There are 88 keys on a keyboard, the voice would be the 89th.

elbow: one pound of marijuana.

electric boogaloo: a break dance.

E-MC's/cyber MC's: online emcees.

Eminem: Marshall Mathers. Rapper. Detroit native. Member of D12. Holds record for selling 1.76 million copies in first week. A.k.a. Slim Shady.

ends: money.

ENYCE: hip-hop clothing line. "ENYCE" is the phonetic spelling for NYC.

ep: extended-play album.

eq: equalizer.

Esham: Esham Smith. Indie rapper credited for putting Detroit on the hip-hop music scene.

E.T. marijuana.

Eve: Eve Jeffers. Rapper known as the "first lady of Ruff Ryder" records. She's called a pit bull in a skirt.

everything is sunny: all is well.

ex-factor: anything unaccounted for; a variable.

extensions: human or synthetic hair braided or sewn into a person's natural hair to give length or volume.

extra: Overboard; to the extreme. "He be on some *extra* shit, talking madd trash."

eyegasm/eye candy: 1) pretty girl. 2) pleasing to the sight.

E-Z Widers: extra-wide rolling paper for tobacco or marijuana.

fa': for. "I'm here *fa'* ya babe."

fab: fabulous; also "fabou."

Fab Five Freddy: Fred Braithwaite, original host of *Yo' MTV Raps!,* the show that took rap to the mainstream.

face-cracked: embarrassed.

face the noise: to endure the consequences.

fade: 1) haircut faded on the sides. 2) to kill. 3) to leave.

faded: 1) drugged by choice or chance. 2) outdated.

fag: male homosexual (offensive).

fag hag: female who often hangs with male homosexuals.

fair-to-middling: okay status.

Faith Evans: Songstress. Sings the R&B hook in many hip-hop songs. Known as the "first lady of Bad Boy Records," P. Diddy's record company. The widow of Notorious B.I.G.

fakin' the funk: pretending.

fam: term of familiar address, as in family.

family: 1) relatives or close friends. "We *family*, we shouldn't be acting like this." 2) statement of inclusion. "He with me, he *family*, y'all don't have to worry about him."

fannie: butt.

fanzines: magazines (any type).

fa' real dough: for real though. It's a statement by a person not convinced of what he's being told.

fa' sho: for sure.

fat: good.

fat beats: nice music.

fat on the hog: prosperous.

fa' true: for true.

fatty girl: pretty girl.

faulty: flawed.

feature: 1) to pay attention to. "I'm not *featuring* him this week. 2) guest artist on a record.

Fed: federal prison.

Feds: federal government.

FEDS: acronym for hip-hop magazine, which means Finally Every Dimension of the Streets.

feedin' (off of someone else): benefiting from someone else's style.

feelin' it: mental connection.

feel me: understand me.

feenin'/feendin': craving.

fend for: defend, support, take care of. "We had to *fend for* ourselves growin' up."

fell off: 1) dropped in record sales. 2) dropped out of sight. 3) not as good as before. 4) not as popular.

FELON: acronym for hip-hop magazine which means, From Every Level of Neighborhoods.

fem: 1) female, feminine. 2) a girly male.

female MC: female rapper. Female MCs, with the exception of a few, dressed like their male counterparts and rapped hard-core to gain respect in the hip-hop industry; some of the current female MCs mix hard-core and sexy image with their skilled delivery.

fetti: money.

fiber-optic battle: online MC battle.

fichola: it's all good. (Cape Verde)

fiddles: no good.

fiend: to have strong desire for.

fierce: beyond reproach.

fifteen minutes: sudden fame that doesn't last.

fifth ward: New Orleans government-assisted housing area. (LA)

fifty-one: mixture of marijuana and cocaine, a.k.a. cabby. (CA)

fill up: to get gasoline for a car.

filthy: lots of money.

fine: 1) nice shape and pretty face. 2) nice body with sexy features. 3) okay, all right, I agree. "That's *fine*."

finger dancing: deejaying.

fin'na: fixing to (do something). "I'm *fin'na* go."

fish scale: good, meaning raw and uncut.

Five Boroughs (of New York): Manhattan, Bronx, Brooklyn, Queens, Staten Island.

5x10: jail cell.

five-finger discount: stealing. "He got that on the *five-finger discount*."

Five-O: police, as in *Hawaii Five-O*.

five-on-five: basketball.

five on it: a contribution of five dollars for a bill. The price of a nickel bag of weed—$5.

fix: a hit of drugs.

flake: ambivalent person, not one to be trusted.

flame: flamboyant homosexual.

flame-thrower: rapper with good lyrical skills.

flares: a break dance.

flash: switch up attitude. "He got around his boys and the nigga *flashed* on me."

flash in the pan: one-hit wonder, so to speak. A person who left as quickly as they came.

flat: dead.

flava: flavor—style.

flexing: flaunting.

flick: movie.

flip/flip lip: smart-mouthed person.

flip loot: 1) to make money. 2) to use illegal money to start legitimate business.

Flipmode Squad: rapper Busta Rhymes's colorful team of hip-hop hype-men/women and MCs.

flipped out: sudden change in behavior, usually negative.

flip stacks: to sell records.

flip the script: to change, switch.

flix/flicks: 1) graffiti. 2) movie or TV show. "What channel the kung-fu *flicks* comin' on?"

floored: outdone, overwhelmed. "When I found out Biggie was dead, it *floored* me."

floozy: 1) stripper. 2) whore.

flossin': flaunting, boasting, bragging.

flow: 1) money. 2) to rap smoothly, fluidly. 3) to have continuity.

flower: feminine lesbian.

flowers: marijuana.

flow-motion: movement in virtual reality game—it flows smoothly.

fly: exceptional. "That suit he has on is *fly*."

fo-fo/four: forty-four-magnum handgun.

food for thought: information to ponder.

foogazy: 1) homosexual. 2) bullshit.

for real, for real: I'm really serious

forty acres and a mule: The supposed compensation from the U.S. government to African Americans when slavery ended.

forty/forty dog: forty ounces of beer.

fou-fou/frou-frou: fancy.

four elements of hip-hop: 1) deejaying. 2) break dancing. 3) emceeing. 4) writing (graffiti).

four-twenty: marijuana.

Foxy Brown: Inga Marchand. Female MC who uses feminine sexuality to sell records. Coined term "il na-na." It suggests vagina but according to reports Marchand says "Ill Na Na" is her nickname.

freak: 1) sexually charged or sexually aggressive person. 2) to wear. "I'm a *freak* this outfit tonight."

freak it: 1) to do well. 2) to make something look good. "I think I'm a *freak* this jacket tonight."

Freaknic: annual picnic held in Atlanta, Georgia, attended by Black college students from across the country. Started at Morehouse College as annual picnic for Atlanta University Center students from the DC metro area.

freestyle: unrehearsed, stream-of-consciousness rap.

Fresh Prince: Will Smith. Rapper, actor. Among first rappers not to use profanity, violence, and misogyny in his raps. Also, one of the first rappers to cross over into acting. He brought hip-hop to the small screen with *The Fresh Prince of Bel-Air* (see **hip-hop television**).

fresh: innovative, new.

friend-girl: noncommittal name given to an intimate female friend as opposed to calling her a girlfriend.

front: 1) pretend. 2) take care of. "I'll *front* you."

front man: lead rapper in a group.

fronts: gold front teeth.

frost: diamond.

frostbite: (wearing) lots of diamond jewelry.

fruit loop: crazy person or person acting like they may be certifiable.

FUBU: acronym for hip-hop clothing design team that stands for For Us By Us. Black-owned hip-hop clothing line.

fucked: 1) harmed in some way. 2) in a lot of trouble.

fugasi: bullshit.

fugly: especially ugly, combination of fucking ugly. "That mofo is *fugly*."

fuhgidabowdit: forget about it.

full: 1) highly emotional. 2) drunk.

funk: soulful groove music with spacey rock and blues sound created by George Clinton and the Parliament in the '70s (see **P-Funk**).

funkdafied: funk-filled and fun.

Funkmaster Flex: Aston Taylor. DJ, business executive. Legendary New York radio personality. Known for playing exclusive hip-hop tracks. Said to be able to make or break a song with radio play. First regular hip-hop DJ on NYC and L.A. radio stations.

funk music: soulful, spirited music with live instrumentation. Music with good groove, good vibe.

funk workouts: sex.

funky: 1) stinky. 2) soulful-sounding groove music.

funky-fresh: innovative look or idea.

future: salutation.

future funk: borrows from alternative music source to heighten hip-hop vibe without losing its groove.

fuzz: 1) police. 2) pubic hair.

FYBISLM: an acronym: f#&! yo bitch if she let me. (MI)

F.Y.I.: for your information.

G-Spot: sexual pleasure zone.

G: 1) God. 2) gangster. 3) grand, as in one thousand dollars. 4) game, which refers to life (see **game**).

game: 1) charm, intelligence, or manipulative ability. 2) young black male, too often a synonym for criminal thug or predator. 3) a business of any kind. 4) life/thug life. 5) willing. "I'm *game*."

gang-banger/bangin': 1) group fights. 2) group sex.

gangsta glam: gangster glamorized in high fashion and style.

gangsta lean: relaxed, cool look.

gangsta rap: rap songs of murder, money, and mayhem. Describes sex, drugs, and violence in detail. Elements of danger, profanity, and black machismo.

gangstress: a female gang member.

ganja: marijuana.

gank: 1) to take for a fool. 2) to beat.

garbage: not good.

garlic: music or lyrics with good sound (full of flavor).

gash: insult.

gassed: 1) high on drugs. 2) excited.

gat: gun.

gazelles (Cazalles?): expensive style of glasses made popular in the 1980s.

g'd: dressed up. Short for "G" in *GQ* magazine.

gear: clothes.

geek: person without style.

geeked up: amped up, excited. (MI)

geo: geography, region, or place where one lives. Most artists rep where they are from. "I was never no *geo* ass nigga."

get a grip: take control.

get at me (dog/dawg): 1) get in touch with me. 2) fight.

get busy: 1) have sex. 2) start.

get down: 1) enjoy. 2) have sex.

get got: threatened to be defeated.

get in that ass: threaten to harm.

get it how you live it: hustle.

get it on: refers to any kind of action, i.e., to fight, have sex, etc. "We 'bout to *get it on*."

get open: receptive.

get paid: get money, legally or illegally.

getting over: benefiting without putting in the labor.

get-up: outfit. "He's wearing a tight *get-up*."

get up on this: a challenge.

get with the program/game: stop slacking, get involved.

get with you: 1) to have an intimate moment. "I want to *get with you.*"
2) threaten to fight.

get your groove on: to have a good time, usually in a sexual sense.

get your lean on: cruising in freshly washed car.

get your swell/swerve on: (see **get your groove on**).

G-4: private jet.

g-funk: gangster funk—long, slow grooves with reggae or soulful sounds
and gangster lyrics.

ghetto: 1) government-assisted living area or a neighborhood that is bro-
ken down due to crime and poor economic conditions. 2) inner city.
3) temporary holding grounds for European Jews who were to be ex-
terminated by Nazis. 4) low quality. 5) unconquerable spirit that exists despite the obvious oppression. 6) unsophisticated Black person.

ghetto bird: police helicopter.

ghetto-cheese: big block of thick, uncut American cheese issued by the
government to people on welfare. It is the best cheese for making
macaroni and cheese.

ghetto-chic: a person from a (Black) ghetto who tries makes a cheap outfit look good.

ghetto-fabulous: a stylish or flashy person from the (Black) ghetto.

ghetto fantasy: wish to move from impoverished state into a better, more
luxurious lifestyle.

ghetto-girl: female ignorant to establishment ways.

ghetto-griot: 1) inner-city poet. 2) a rapper.

ghetto-grit: 1) rough and raw behavior. 2) the unconquerable spirit of the ghetto that allows for creative juices to flow.

ghetto-queen: 1) Black mothers who live in the inner cities and who struggle to feed their children. 2) girlfriend, who usually lives in the inner city.

ghetto-superstar: person from the inner city who achieves success locally (usually a small-time or neighborhood drug dealer).

ghost: 1) absent, dead or alive. 2) to leave. 3) ghostwriter.

gig/gigging: 1) job. 2) party; having a good time.

gimme: give me.

gimme five: request for a single hand slap as a gesture of agreement or encouragement.

girlfriend: term of familiar address used in small talk, usually among girls.

give up the ghost: die.

giving kicks and snares: the appreciation of beats or instruments that add new sound to music.

giving the eye: flirting.

givin' it up: 1) looking good. 2) giving in to sexual desires. "She be *giving it up* to everybody."

glock: gun.

glory: 1) body. "That girl is showing all her *glory*, titties, and ass everywhere!" 2) talent.

g-money: 1) gangster money. Money that is earned illegally. 2) term of familiar address.

go: an encouraging word. "You *go*, boy!"

go bananas: acting out of control.

go down/go down south/go downtown: perform oral sex.

God: 1) controlling spiritual force. 2) awesome lyricist, writer, deejay, breaker.

go for broke: risk it all.

gold-digger: person seeking the riches of another. "Watch ya pockets yo, she a *gold-digger*."

golden: fresh, new, clean.

golden boy/girl: an artist (or group) who sells 500,000 copies of a record or album. Selling half a million records puts him/her at gold record status.

golden showers: pee, as in piss on.

good book: the *Holy Bible*.

goodfella rich: rich from drug trade.

good hair: straight or soft curly hair as opposed to kinky or hard, nappy hair.

good looking: good-looking out.

goods: assets.

good to go: 1) ready, prepared. 2) pleasing.

goose chasin': pursuit without result.

gorgerific: the combination of the two terms gorgeous and terrific.

Gorillaz: twenty-first-century multicultural animated pop group much like the Archies with Archie, Veronica, Jughead, et al.

got it going on: doing well.

got your back: pledge to support.

government cheese: (see **ghetto-cheese**).

government handle/title: registered birth name.

g.p.: general principle, to follow the established rule as the reason for action.

graffiti: an artform usually displayed on public facades that features brilliant colors and cryptic intricacy. An expression of art often considered a public nuisance because the canvases are public spaces—subways, handball courts, and buildings. Artists insist they're enhancing the spectrum.

graffiti ergo sum: "I write therefore I am." The saying of graf writer Cartesian Phil.

graf kats: graffiti writers.

grain: overproof alcoholic beverage, usually mixed with Kool-Aid for consumption.

Grandmaster Flash: Joseph Saddler, rapper. Raised the level of social commentary in rap. He created the back spinning DJ technique.

Grandmaster Flash and the Furious Five: first rap super group. Grandmaster Flash (Joseph Saddler), Raheim (Guy Williams), Melle Mel (Melvin Glover), Kid Creole (Nathaniel Glover, Melle Mel's brother), Mr. Ness (Eddie Morris), Cowboy (Keith Wiggins).

Grand Puba: leader.

Grand Wizard Theodore: Theodore Livingston, DJ. Invented the scratch technique or scratch music—sliding the needle on a record to create new sound.

grapevine: human gossip chain.

gratta: pants stuck in the butt.

gravy: 1) the extras, compare this to saying "the icing on the cake." 2) a response that means good. "How is everything?" Response: "Everything is *gravy*."

green guys: money.

green leaves: marijuana.

greenthumb: marijuana grower.

grill: 1) teeth cover, usually made of gold and diamonds. 2) steel protective frame for a vehicle. 3) face.

grimey: 1) unkempt. 2) struggling, but trying.

grinding: selling/hustling.

griot: poet/lyricist.

grip: 1) money. 2) to drive a car. 3) to grab.

grit licks: gritty lyrics.

groove: 1) to have a good time. 2) mellow.

gul/guhl: girl.

gully: 1) liar. 2) common, ordinary.

gumbo: 1) spicy soup with shrimp and okra. 2) a dialect spoken by some Blacks, and Creoles in Louisiana and the French West Indies.

gump: person lacking poise and good posture.

gunning: to attack verbally or physically.

gut: have sex with; penetrate deeply. "I *gutted* her out last night."

gutter/guttah: low state of being.

g.w.p. (gift with purchase): a gift that comes with the purchase of an item.

gym shoes: sport shoes.

ha!: affirmation/exclamation. (DS)

hair-do: hairstyle.

hair don't: bad hairstyle.

half steppin': failing to complete; lazy.

ham it up: to have fun.

Hammerman: hip-hop cartoon based on rapper MC Hammer.

handball: A sport in which hands are used to hit a ball against a wall.

handle: name; can be registered birthname or self-given name. "What's ya *handle*, bruh?"

handles: athletic footwear. Also called gym shoes or sneakers.

handle your business: 1) take care of your business. 2) suggestion to mind your own business.

happy camper: jovial person.

hard: 1) mean. 2) physically strong. 3) erect. 4) one who has had to struggle to survive.

hard-core: 1) grim reflections of the struggle to survive oppression. 2) violent or sexually explicit lyrics.

hard-knock life: life of struggle.

Harlem Shake: a dance in which one alternates the movement of the shoulders in sync with music.

hater/hata: jealous person.

hateration: hating.

hawk: 1) check out. 2) cold winter air. "That Detroit *hawk* is kicking."

head: 1) person. 2) oral sex performed on a male.

head bopper: song that makes you move to a rhythm not your own.

head buster: fighter.

head case: crazy person.

head-cracker: tough decision.

head gear: anything used to cover the head.

heads/headz: people.

heads up: be aware, look out

heart stopper: to penetrate someone with iron—shoot and kill with gun. (DS)

heat/heater: 1) gun. 2) police. 3) good output. "He bringing the *heat* on the song."

heated: extremely angry.

heat pad: writing pad—battleground where lyricists work out their aggression and deal with the reality of their blues.

Heavy D: Dwight Myers. Rapper, actor. Calls himself heavy because he is overweight. Low-key rapper known for putting out consistently good music and witty rhymes.

hebies: 1) loose crack. 2) any sexual disease. 3) feeling of repugnance. "He gives me the *hebies*."

hella: 1) hell of, which means remarkable. "He got on some *hella* gear." 2) a lot.

hello: used to concur with something that has been said.

Henry: Hennessy (cognac).

herb: 1) nerd. 2) marijuana.

hey foya: what's up, shawty? (Cape Verde)

heyy, ho/heyyo: party chant.

H.H.I.C.: Head Honey In Charge, from the featured section in *Honey*, a magazine for young African American women.

hick: person who behaves in Southern manner and style (offensive).

hickey: mark created from sucking hard on the body during intimacy.

higglers: street vendors. (Jamaica)

high: 1) feeling the effects of drugs. 2) having a good time.

high beaming: successful; like high beams on cars, person is said to be high beaming when they are doing well.

high 5/5 high: hand slap.

high-hop: a hip-hop style of music created by Dr. Cornell West, African American Studies Professor at Harvard University, that speaks to the mind and not the material.

high maintenance: needy.

highsidin': 1) acting snobby. 2) boasting.

high-top fade: haircut, high on top, low on sides.

high-tops: sport shoes with added material for ankle support.

hip: 1) trendy. 2) to agree. "I'm *hip*."

hip-hop: the artistic response to oppression. A way of expression in dance, music, word/song. A culture that thrives on creativity and nostalgia. As a musical art form it is stories of inner-city life, often with a message, spoken over beats of music. The culture includes rap and any other venture spawned from the hip-hop style and culture.

hip-hop books:
Ego Tripp's Book of Rap Lists
Hip-Hop America
King Rock
Nation's Conscious Rap: The Hip-Hop Vision
Situations
Street Conscious Rap
Street Kingdom: Five Years Inside the Franklin Avenue Posse
Tha Doggfather
The Vibe History of Hip-Hop
Twisted Tales in the Hip-Hop Streets of Philly

hip-hop comics and artists:
The Boondocks, by Aaron McGruder
Iceberg Slick
Urbanstylecomics.com

hip-hop diamond: an artist who sells 10 million plus of one record or album (see **diamond**).

hip-hop drinks: (See your local bartender for ingredients. You must be twenty-one to drink.)
Alize
Beautiful
Blood
Chocolate Shake

Cutie
Ghetto Viagra
Gin and juice
Guerrilla Milk
Makaveli
Num Num juice
Real Love
Sweet Thing
Thug Passion

hip-hop fashion:
Baby Phat
Blackfokapparel/Blackfokapparel.com
Bushi
Clark's
Damani Dada
Dupri Styles
FJ560
FUBU
Kalonjiwear
Karl Kani
Lugz
Mecca USA
Napp
No Limit
Outkast Clothing
Parasuco
Phat Farm
Roc-A-Fella
Sean John
Skecher's
Timberlands
Triple 5 Soul
vokal
Wally's
Wu-wear

hip-hop fiends: die-hard hip-hop fans.

a
b
c
d
e
f
g

i
j
k
l
m
n
o
p
q
r
s
t
u
v
w
x
y
z

hip-hop funk: the combination of funk or soulful music and hip-hop lyrics. Also called hip-hop soul.

hip-hop graphix Cos: Pen & Pixel, Phunky Phat Graphics, Street Level Graphics.

hip-hop guru: well-respected person in one of the four elements of hip-hop.

hip-hop heads: the people of the hip-hop culture.

hip-hop hippies: socially conscious rap music makers and their fans.

hip-hop magazines:
Beatdown, rap's first newspaper.
Don Diva
FEDS
FELON
Front
Mo' Cheez
Murder Dog
One Nutt
Rap Pages
Rap Sheet
Rap-up Magazine
Right On Magazine.
Stress
The Fader
The Source, first hip-hop magazine. Published 1988.
Trix (UK)
URB
Vibe
XXL

hip-hop movies:
Above the Rim
Beat Street
Belly
Blazin'
Breakin'

Bulworth
Crime Partners
Exit Wounds
Flashdance
Freestyle
Friday 1, 2
Gang Related
High School High
House Party
How High
Juice
Krush Groove
Menace to Society
New Jack City
Prince Among Thieves
Rage
Rapstresses
Rhyme and Reason
Scratch: a DJ documentary
Set It Off
Slam
Soul in the Hole
State Property
Stations of the Elevated
Style Wars
The Crow Lazarus
The Wash
Thicker Than Water
Turn It Up
Wave Twisters—hip-hop's first animated full-length feature film by DJ Q-Bert.
Wild Style
Who's the Man

hip-hop play: hip-hop gospel play, *If the fly on the wall could talk.*

hip-hop record companies:
Aftermath
BMG (Bertlesmann Music Group): RCA, Arista, Jive.

Cash Money
Coroner
Detonator
EMD (EMI): Virgin, Capitol, EMI, Priority.
Enjoy
Flava Unit
Hoo-Bangin'
No Limit
Profile
Rap-A-Lot
Rawkus
Roc-A-Fella
Ruff Ryders
Ruffhouse
Ruthless
Sony: Columbia, So So Def, 550, Epic, Loud, Bad Boy.
Sugar Hill
Tommy Boy
UMG (Universal Music Group): Universal, Island, Def Jam, Polygram, Interscope, Motown, MCA.
Untertainment
WEA (Warner, Elektra, Atlantic): Warner, Elektra, Atlantic.

hip-hopreneurs: hip-hop entrepreneurs.

hip-hop siren: female who sings the R&B chorus or hook on a hip-hop record.

hip-hop soul: hip-hop music with a soulful sound.

hip-hop television:
 The Fresh Prince of Bel-Air
 Homeboys in Outer Space
 In the House
 Living Single
 Moesha

hip-hop theater: the unleashing of words and concepts into action onstage.

hip-hop websites:

360hiphop.com
AKA.com
Allmusic.com
Breakdancing.com
Crosswinds.net (lyrics)
Dalinkwent.com
Daplyrics.com
EURweb.com
Fanfam.com
Freestyling.com
Hiphophut.com
Hip-hoptionary.com
Hookt.com
Hookt.com
Kumba-kali.com (African)
LeHiphop.com (French)
lyrics.com
Ohhla.com
Peeps.com
Platform.net
Platform.net
Rapnetwork.com
Rapstation.com
rap-up.com
Thefader.com
Ughh.com

hip-pop: commercially driven hip-hop.

hit: 1) to have sex. 2) ugly person. "She *hit*."

hit and run: one-night stand. "I did a *hit and run* on that honey the other night."

hit 'em up: 1) ask. 2) take someone's money.

hit me up: call me.

hit me on the hip: call me on my cell phone.

hit squad: 1) record company's team of musicians. 2) team of criminals, bounty hunters.

hit that lick: good luck. (TX)

hit you up: 1) to call. 2) to seek a favor from. "Can I *hit you up* for a couple of dollars until next week?"

hittin': on target. "That sex was *hittin'*."

hittin' switches: taking lives, killing.

hitting/working the block: hustling, selling drugs.

hivestock: a "hip-hop Woodstock" in Tampa, Florida, organized by the Tampa hip-hop magazine *The Hive*.

ho': 1) whore. 2) coward.

ho-car: signal to tell prostitutes police are coming.

hold down the fort: take care of things while I'm gone.

hold it down: keep things in order.

hold your own: take care of self.

hole: vagina.

holla (back): 1) talk to you later. 2) call me.

hollyhood: glamorous gangster.

hollywood: 1) person who seeks the trappings of beauty, fame, and fortune. 2) stylish person. 3) liar, person who tells tall tales.

homeboy/homegirl/homey/homies/home slice/home skillet: 1) term of familiar address. **2)** reference to a person from the same neighborhood or hometown.

homefront: home.

homo-thug: usually bisexual male, but one can't tell if he is homo.

honey: 1) pretty girl. 2) hip-hop magazine for females.

honey dip: pretty girl.

honkey: white person (offensive). Term comes from white men who would honk their horns in the inner city to get a prostitute's attention.

'hood: neighborhood.

'hood rat: person often seen aimlessly hanging around a neighborhood.

'hoodies: the people from a neighborhood.

hoodwinked: tricked (attributed to Malcolm X).

hoody: sweatshirt with hood attached.

hook: 1) repeated verse in a song. 2) to trade sex for money.

hook me up: do me a favor.

hook(ed)-up: 1) to get together with another. 2) do a favor or good deed for someone. "She *hooked* him up with a house after she made it big." 3) well connected.

hoop dreams: dreams of being a professional basketball player.

hooptie: raggedy car.

horn: 1) telephone. 2) crack cocaine. "She blowin' that *horn*, yo."

horrorcore rap: rap with themes of horror, dead bodies, funerals, tombs, etc.

hoss: term of familiar address.

hot: 1) stolen. 2) to be in possession of drugs. 3) to be sought after by police. 4) good-looking or popular person. 5) item that sells well. 6) anything good.

hot-block: neighborhood street with illegal activity going on.

hot-boy: 1) a guy who likes nice things and having fun but who also is goal oriented. 2) attractive male. 3) pretty boy thug. (LA)

hot flashes: symptoms of menopause.

hot-girl: attractive female.

hothead: quick-tempered.

Hotlanta: Atlanta, Georgia.

hot-n-bothered: sexually excited or frustrated.

hot-spot: 1) vagina. 2) happening scene.

hottie: pretty girl.

hot-to-death: very good. "Fabolous' Holla Back is *hot-to-death*."

house/house music: music with a focus on vibe and atmosphere and with great dance beats.

house nigga: Black person who lives by the rules of the white establishment.

house party: party inside someone's house.

H.N.I.C.: Head Nigger In Charge. The person can be white or Black.

H-Town: Houston, Texas.

hug drug: ecstasy.

human beat box: ability to make instrumental sounds using the mouth.

hummer'n 'em: living well, suggesting ability to drive the expensive Hummer vehicle.

humming: stinking, smelly.

hump day: Wednesday, the middle of the five-day work week.

hun/hunn'ed: hundred-dollar bill.

hung: endowed male.

hurt: ugly. "His face is *hurt*."

hush-hush: secret gossip, if there is such a thing. "That's supposed to be *hush-hush*, so don't tell nobody."

hustler: 1) hardworking, clever moneymaker. 2) male prostitute.

hydraulics: make car go up and down. It's a way of communicating in certain areas of L.A. Riding low means no trouble. Riding high means beef. (CA)

hydro: marijuana that is chemically enhanced to make it more potent.

hydro foil: land-water vehicle.

hygienic lyricist: clean-cut rapper.

hype: 1) propaganda. 2) amazing.

hype-man: person who excites a crowd and keeps a party going by shouting call-and-response chants on a microphone like, "heyy, ho!" or "the roof, the roof, the roof is on fire. We don't need no water let the motherfucker burn, burn motherfucker burn!"

Hype Williams: hip-hop music video director.

I ain't feeling that: to oppose or dislike something.

I ain't mad at cha': a compliment to someone who has succeeded.

I ain't the one: don't mess with me.

ice: 1) diamonds. 2) dead. 3) drugs. 4) kill. 5) good.

Iceberg Slim: author of pimp stories.

ice cream: cocaine.

Ice Cube: O'Shea Jackson. Rapper, actor, writer, director. Solo rapper, also member of N.W.A. (Niggas With Attitude). Cube was among the first to do hip-hop films.

ice-grill: 1) stare. 2) frown.

Ice T: Tracey Morrow. Rapper, actor, author, business executive. Raps about street hustling and street survival. One of his songs, "Cop Killer," put him in direct battle with the federal government. Ice had the first rap album to carry a warning label. Created a dictionary of pimp lingo called *Pimptionary*.

I feel you: I understand you.

If I say it it's platinum: you have my word.

IFPI: International Federation of the Phonographic, represents the international recording industry and keeps track of records sales worldwide.

Iladelph: Philadelphia, Pennsylvania. A.k.a. Philly.

il da-da/il pa-pa: penis.

il na-na: 1) vagina. 2) little Mami, Foxy Brown's nickname.

I got you: I'll take care of you.

I got your back: I will support your endeavor.

I'm good: I'm okay.

ig'nant: ignorant.

ill/illin: 1) weird/strange. 2) good. 3) not good.

illegal: great.

illiest: best.

illmatic: 1) drugs. 2) rapper, Nas.

illo: illustration.

Ill-Town: East Orange, New Jersey.

I'mma: going to do something. "*I'mma* get me one of those when I make it big."

I'm out/outti: I'm leaving; see you later.

imp: impostor; pretentious person.

Impala: Chevrolet automobile. Popular car among West Coast/gangster rappers.

in a minute: good-bye.

Indie: 1) independent. 2) independent promoter—music consultant to radio program director.

a
b
c
d
e
f
g
h
> i
j
k
l
m
n
o
p
q
r
s
t
u
v
w
x
y
z

indo/endo: marijuana.

in full effect: 1) happening as we speak. 2) full representation or complete.

in jump: keeping moving/dancing. "That record got e'rbody *in jump*."

inner-city dwellers: urban residents.

in the buck: traditional sexual position.

in the cut: 1) having sex. 2) at home. 3) behind the scenes.

in the mix: to be a part of an event or occurrence, positive or negative. "She got caught up *in the mix*."

Independent Distributors: cos that distribute locally made records regularly and nationally for independent artists or major record cos, such as Select O Hits (Memphis), Bay City Hall (Bay Area), Southwest Wholesale (Houston).

Iraq: LeFrak, New York.

iron: 1) gun. 2) weights.

ish: chitchat. "We sat around shooting the *ish*."

isht: expletive, like shit.

-isms: negative things like racism, classism, sexism.

issues: problems. "Don't fuck with her, man, she got mad *issues*."

it: 1) the latest trend in song, dance, people, etc. "She's the new *it* girl." 2) sex. "They did *it* last night." 3) any object or thing when speaking in coded language.

it's a wrap: finished.

it's all good: no problems.

it's on: 1) agreement to act on something. 2) it's about to happen. 3) it's on target.

izzo, izza language: Pig latin, a communal language spoken by Black people to code their message. Jay Z uses izzo language in his song "HOVA" when he says, "H to the izzO, V to the izzA," which spells his name H-O-V-A.

j: joint, marijuana cigarette.

jack: 1) steal, rob. 2) empty, zero, nothing. "I ain't got *jack* until the first of the month."

Jacob the Jeweler: jewelry maker.

Jah: God. (Jamaica)

Jake: police.

jam: 1) to dance well. 2) a party. 3) a good song. "That song is the *jam.*" 4) trapped. "I got *jammed* up in that mess."

jammy: 1) situation. 2) a black eye received from a punch.

jane doe: average or unknown female.

jank: good. (VA)

jawn: penis.

Jay-Z: Shawn Carter. Rapper, entrepreneur. Brooklyn native. Considered one of the best, if not the best, rapper. Fluid raps. Consistently good. Often boasts of having vast knowledge, riches, and rap skills. A.k.a. Jigga, King Hova.

Jazz-rap: hip-hop that embodies elements of jazz.

Jean-Michel Basquiat: an Andy Warhol protégé who became famous for his graffiti-inspired art.

Jedi mind-tricks: what you see isn't real.

jerkin' beef: 1) wasting time. 2) pretending. 3) masturbating.

Jermaine Dupri: Jermaine Dupri Mauldin. Producer, rapper. One of hip-hop's youngest executives and best music producers. Owns So-So Def Records.

jet: leave.

jewel(s): 1) a verse in a song that offers knowledge, wisdom. 2) a recording artist who makes money for his company. 3) testicles.

Jheri Curl: processed curly hair.

jiggy: clean-cut and bouncy-fun.

jime/jimmy: penis.

jimmy hat: condom.

jing: money.

jit: 1) drug dealer. 2) a type of dance, jitterbug.

jitney: bootleg cab driver.

J.O.: job, as in j-o-b.

jock(ing): overly and obviously friendly, perhaps for something in return.

joe: average.

Johnny Nunez: hip-hop photographer of choice. Nunez created first line of hip-hop greeting cards.

johnny pump: fire hydrant. "Somebody needs to call the fire department to open the *johnny pumps* so niggas can cool off."

johnson: penis.

joint: 1) marijuana cigarette. 2) location. "Let's head over to his *joint*." 3) record. 4) can reference anything in a positive way. "That smoke is the *joint*." "That outfit is the *joint*."

jone: poke fun at, jokingly insult.

jonesing: living nicely.

Jones's: 1) the copycat standard. 2) crave. "I still got the *Jones's* for my ex."

Jont: stuff.

jook(ed): 1) to scam, trick, or dupe. 2) to stab with a knife.

J.P.T.: Japanese People Time, which generally is early.

judy fly: marijuana cigarette laced with crack cocaine.

juice: 1) power. "That new promotion gave him some *juice*." 2) gun. 3) outpace. 4) alcoholic beverage.

jump: good. "That CD is *jump*."

jump off: about to happen.

jump-street: the start.

junk in the trunk: big butt.

>>> **k**

Kamikaze: direct, hard, all out.

Kangol: hat manufacturer.

karena: pretty girl.

Karl Kani: Carl Williams. Designer. Among the first to create a hip-hop clothing line. Known as the Godfather of urban fashion.

keepin' it real: living honestly.

keep it light: keep things safe, fair, and easy.

keep it real: tell the truth.

keep it tight: don't mess things up.

key: 1) measurement for cocaine. 2) type. 3) connection. "I got the *key* to your heart."

key-stylin': online MC battlers who type their lyrics in the computer keyboard.

kick (it): 1) perform. 2) indulge in a relationship.

kickin': 1) dating. 2) anything that is pleasing. 3) bad smell.

kicking rocks: hanging out.

kick it to you: 1) pass along. 2) initial approach when trying to make someone your girlfriend.

kicks: shoes.

kick to the curb: quit.

kil: guy. (Netherlands)

killed it: did a good job.

killer: 1) a person with good taste or style. 2) anything pleasing, good. 3) ladies' man.

killin' it: doing well.

killin' me: 1) making someone laugh. 2) fall short of accomplishment.

kill that shit: put an end to what you're doing.

kiss: drugs.

kite: letter.

kite/kike: people of Jewish faith (offensive).

kitty-cat: vagina.

knahmsayin: know what I'm saying?; also knahmean.

knee pads: a metaphor for giving someone a blow job or being an ass kisser.

knob: penis.

knocked up: pregnant.

knockin' the boots: having sex.

knot: money.

knowledge me: inform me.

knuckle-up: fight.

Kool-Aid smile: huge smile, usually wider than necessary. "I gave my little sister a dollar and she walks to the candy store with a *Kool-Aid smile* on her face."

Kool DJ Here: Clive Campbell. DJ. Known as the father of hip-hop. Credited with creating the hip-hop sound in 1971. Called the original DJ.

kosher dutch: it's all good. (IN)

KRS One: Lawrence "Kris" Parker. Rapper, author. Known as one of the original "edutainers" of rap—one who educates and entertains. Often called the most skillful lyrical battlers in rap music. His rap style challenged stereotypical thinking and showed the intellectual side of rap. KRS One is an acronym that means Knowledge Reigns Supreme Over Nearly Everyone.

krushin': pleasing.

Krylon: spray-paint manufacturer—brand made popular by graffiti artists.

K-tone: gun.

Kumba-Kali.com: an African hip-hop Web site.

Kurtis Blow: Kurtis Walker. Rapper. First rapper to sign with major label and first to get a gold record (500,000 record sales) status with rap.

Kuwait: Queensboro, New York.

Kwaito: cross between hip-hop and reggae music sounds. (South Africa)

K-Y Jelly: vaginal lubricant.

L: 1) blunt/marijuana. 2) money. 3) loss, as in "You'll have to take that *L*, son."

la: marijuana.

lab: recording studio.

'Lac: Cadillac. Luxury General Motors vehicle.

lace (d): 1) mixed, intertwined. 2) draped in jewels. 3) to provide for.

Lambo: Lamborghini vehicle.

lame: no good.

lampin': hanging out, like a streetlamp, in the neighborhood.

land: Land Rover sports utility vehicle.

large: successful.

late: 1) behind the times. 2) no good (see **tired**).

lauw: rhymes with how and means pretty good. (Netherlands)

lay low: keep a low profile.

lay pipe: sexually penetrate.

LBC: Long Beach City, California.

L-Boogie: Lauryn Hill. Rapper, singer, producer, actress. Member of The Fugees. Credited with taking rap to the level of class and sophistication.

learn me: get to know me.

leek: PCP. A drug.

Left coast: see **West Coast.**

legend in your own mind: ego-tripping.

legit: legitimate.

Left Eye: Lisa Lopes (1971–2002). Rapper. Member of the rap trio TLC, which also included T-Boz & Chilli, the biggest-selling female group of all time. Lopes died in a car crash while vacationing in Honduras.

LeHipHop.com: a French hip-hop Web site.

L'Esprit: brand of Courvoisier called L'Esprit de Courvoisier, $300 a shot, $5,000 a bottle.

lethal: marijuana.

let's get it on: 1) request for sex. 2) request to battle, fight.

let you have it: to tell someone off, set him or her straight.

Lex: Lexus vehicle.

Liberty City: Miami, Florida.

lick: good song.

licks: lyrics/rhymes.

lid: hat.

lifted: high.

lil' daddy/lil' pappa: male

Lil Bow Wow: Shad Gregory Moss. Teenage rap superstar, actor, from Columbus, Ohio. Snoop Dogg gave him his name.

Lil' Kim: Kimberly Jones. Rapper. Credited with liberating female rappers from dressing like boys and rapping hard-core. She uses her femininity to express herself in rap, sometimes with sexually graphic themes. A.k.a. Queen Be, The Notorious K.I.M.

lil' mama: female.

Lil Romeo: Percy Romeo Miller. Young rap sensation and the son of Master P., making them the first father-and-son of hip-hop.

lit: drunk.

Little Black Book: 1) *Holy Bible.* 2) private phone book.

live: 1) good. "That song is all the way *live.*" 2) having a good time.

livin' large: excessive.

L. L. Cool J.: Ladies Love Cool James. James Todd Smith. Veteran rapper, movie and television actor. Helped bring rap to the mainstream. Uses his fame to promote hip-hop. A.k.a. G.O.A.T. (Greatest Of All Time), Uncle L.

'Lo: Polo. Clothing label designed by Ralph Lauren.

loaded: 1) drunk or high on drugs. 2) person with a lot of money.

locced up: hooked up, got together.

lock: 1) a form of handshake where four fingers connect. 2) dreadlock.

lock-down: 1) jail. 2) under the control the control of a partner or spouse. "She got him on *lock-down.*"

loco: crazy.

locs: prisoners.

lolo: girls.

long money: lots of money—long like rabbit ears.

loosies: loose cigarettes out of the box. Sold at stores for twenty-five or fifty cents a piece.

loot/looch: money.

Lou': St. Louis, Missouri.

louie: left-hand turn in a vehicle.

love boat: drugs.

love drug: ecstasy.

lovely: reference to a girl. "Look at that *lovely.*"

love-you time: shared time.

love you to the bone: unconditional, deep-down love.

low down: 1) gossip. 2) scandalous action.

low ridas: cars with hydraulic systems that allow the cars to go up and down. (CA)

low riding: hanging out, cruising on low in a car with a hydraulic system that allows the car to go up and down. (CA)

LP: long-playing album.

Lucifer: hot, good.

Lugz: shoes/boots.

Luke Campbell: Luther Campbell. Rapper. Uses sexually graphic lyrics. He made the Miami bass, booty-shaking music famous. A.k.a. Luke Skywalker.

lunching: 1) acting strange or crazy. 2) missing out.

lyrical gems: crafty rhymes.

lyrical styles of hip-hop: militant (political), gangsta (street survival), bling-bling (money), Bohemian (musically innovative), alterna-rap (disavows violence and misogyny), conscientious (social commentary), Miami booty shake (sex), spiritual (gospel), etc.

Lyricist Lounge: club in New York which is host site for amateur MC battles. Spawned a CD series and a variety show.

M.A.C.: Makeup Arts Cosmetics. Fashion makeup popular among ladies in hip-hop culture.

mack: 1) pimp. 2) charmer. 3) to steal. 4) to sex.

mack daddy: man with multiple girlfriends.

mad: 1) great. "He's sporting some *mad* gear." 2) a large amount. "Dawg got busted carrying *mad* weight at the airport."

mad real: the honest truth.

mad ups: 1) credit, acknowledgment. 2) high jumper (basketball term).

Mafia: power.

Mafioso style: the idea of putting family first.

Magnolia projects: government-assisted housing in New Orleans. (LA)

Magnums: extra-large condoms.

mainlining: 1) starring. 2) shooting heroin directly into the veins.

Main Street: main drag for cruisers in East L.A. (CA)

main squeeze: primary girlfriend. "I got a lot of hoes but that there is my *main squeeze.*"

makin' waves: causing trouble.

Malcolm X: Malcolm Little. Civil rights leader known for his affiliation with the Nation of Islam and for saying "by any means necessary" during his quest for racial equality and justice. Quit the Nation of Islam. Changed his separatist thinking. Started his own movement. Assassinated 1965. A.k.a. Al Hajj Malik Al Shabazz.

male suburban hip-hop style of dress: baggie pants, T-shirt, baseball cap.

mama's boy: 1) man or boy raised by single female parent. 2) man or boy with feminine ways.

Mambo sauce: barbeque sauce, ketchup, and hot sauce—found only in the corner Chinese restaurant for chicken wings.

mamis: girls.

man: term of familiar address. "What's up, *man?*"

mandingo: physically endowed Black male who evokes carnal desires. Name derived from the movie *Mandingo* about a slave and his white mistress.

man-milk: semen.

marbles: money.

Marcy Projects: government-assisted housing in Brooklyn, New York.

marinate: 1) consider. "I got to let that *marinate* for a second before I make a decision." 2) relax.

mark: 1) punk. 2) target. "Stay away from him, he's a *marked* man."

MARTA: the Atlanta railway system. (GA)

Mary/Mary Jane: marijuana.

Mary J. Blige: songstress known as the Queen of Hip-Hop.

mashin': 1) good. (CA) 2) beating. "Them boys oughtta get a good *mashin'* for slapping that girl like that."

Master P: Percy Miller. Rapper, business executive: creator of No Limit records, No Limit Communications, and No Limit clothing; actor, movie producer, professional basketball player, sports agent. Credited with creating a third coast in music to compete with East Coast hip-hop and West Coast rap. Took DS hip-hop mainstream. A.k.a. The Colonel. Master P made it cool to be country.

matrix: jail.

Maxell: audio tape manufacturer, brand most popular for mixed tapes.

maxin': the maximum. "*Maxin'* and relaxin'."

Maybach: custom-designed Mercedes Benz limo, starting at $300K.

MBP: most ballinest playa.

MC/emcee: master of ceremonies—the person who kept a party hyped with call-and-response party chants. The word has become synonymous with rap. A lyricist with skill and passion for the art. A.k.a. microphone controller, message carrier.

MC Hammer: Stanley Kirk Burrell. Rapper. Changed the course of hip-hop to hip-pop with his commercial squeaky-clean raps, creative dance styles, and wardrobe of bare chest and genie pants.

McRecords: mass production of the same kind of commercial records.

meal ticket: a person who is being used by someone else.

mean: good, serious.

Mecca: New York City.

medicine man: drug dealer.

medina: liquid aphrodisiac.

mega: an extremely large amount.

melon: head. "That cat got a big-ass *melon*."

mental jewels: lyrical lessons.

mental nuggets: useful or thought-provoking lyrics, like gold nuggets.

mess/messy: trouble created from gossip.

metaphorplay: the play on words.

meth: marijuana (see **crystal methamphetamine**).

Method Man: Clifford Smith. Rapper. Member of Wu-Tang Clan. Called the nursery rhyme–style rapper because of his phrasing. A.k.a. Shakuan God Allah.

mettle: skills.

m-f/m-f'er: motherfucker.

mia: Miami, Florida.

mias: shoplifting.

Michael Eric Dyson: Columbia University professor. Staunch advocate of hip-hop and its culture.

mickey: aphrodisiac.

Mickey D's: McDonald's, the fast-food restaurant.

mil: million.

mile high club: people part of the few (or many) who have had sex in an airplane while it was flying.

milk: take advantage of. "She *milked* him for his money."

misanthropy: dis of someone out of jealousy.

Miss Thang: girl who acts like she thinks she's cute or better than others.

Missy "Misdemeanor" Elliott: Melissa Elliott. Rapper, producer, music executive, known for swi, swi, switching her style.

mixtape: compilation tape (or more recently, CD) of various artists—the life blood of underground hip-hop and how artists garner street credibility.

mixtape masters: Funkmaster Flex, DJ Clue, Kay Slay, Whoo Kid.

MJ: 1) Michael Jackson, the music legend. 2) Michael Jordan, the legendary basketball star.

MLK: Martin Luther King, Jr. Civil rights leader who united races in the fight for civil rights. Led a protest march on the nation's capital (Washington, DC) in 1963, where he gave his now famous "I Have a Dream" speech. Awarded the Nobel Peace Prize. Assassinated, 1968.

m'man: my man. A term of familiar address.

Mo': Moët champagne.

M.O.B.: Money Over Bitches.

mo' betta: sex.

Mob town: Mobile, Alabama.

mo-fos: motherfuckers.

mojo: 1) penis. 2) power of persuasion. "After I put the *mojo* on her, I'll get what I want."

Mom and Pop shops: local, independent stores, usually Black owned.

Mo-mo: Detroit, The Motor City.

money: 1) cash. 2) term of familiar address. "What's up, *money*, how are you doing?" **3)** reference to a person with lots of style and who looks like he or she has lots of money.

Money, Power, and Respect: hip-hop board game (moneypowerrespect game.com).

money magnet: person with the ability to make money.

money-maker: 1) asset: voice, body, talent, etc. **2)** hustler.

monster: 1) good. "That's a *monster* beat." **2)** bad person, in the negative sense of the word.

moolah: money.

'mote: remote control.

mouf: mouth.

mouthpieces: rappers/MCs.

move: to sell. "He *moved* mega shit cross the border last night."

move me: make me feel something. "That beat doesn't *move me*."

Mr. Big: Ronald Isley.

Mr. Cartoon: hip-hop celebrity tattooist. (CA)

Mr. Magic: first hip-hop radio DJ, Brooklyn, New York.

M's: millions.

MTV: Music Television.

mug: face.

mule: person paid to traffic drugs.

mumbo/mambo sauce: ketchup and hot sauce mixed, usually offered at Chinese restaurants.

murder(ed): to excel over an opponent in a hip-hop competition. "He *murdered* him on the mic."

murder 1's (ones): sunglasses. (CA)

murderous: good. "Pretty Willis is *murderous* with his rap harmony."

musical blue balls: music that leaves you wanting.

Music City: Nashville, Tennessee.

mutt: 1) mixed-breed dog. 2) snitch.

MVP: most valuable poet.

MW: Midwest.

my bad: acknowledging wrongdoing; an apology.

my people/my peeps: family, friends, or fans.

MYOB: mind your own business.

mystery niggas: bustas. (NM)

na' mean: do you know what I mean?

name-droppin': when someone claims to know famous people.

nann: none.

Naptown: Indianapolis, Indiana.

narc: 1) narcotics. 2) police.

narcotic: good.

nasty: good.

Natty: Cincinnati, Ohio.

Nelly: 1) rapper from St. Louis, Missouri. 2) Southern-acting or -sounding person.

n'em: them.

Neptunes: producers.

new jack: new artist or someone new to a scene.

New Jack City: urban survival story. Among the first in hip-hop movies.

New Jack Swing: HH with groove. Producer Teddy Riley credited with creating New Jack Swing.

New Jeru: New Jersey.

New Jill Swing: female version of New Jack Swing, i.e., TLC.

new school/new skool: any music or artists that came after the advent of drum machines and synthesizers. Conversely, *old school* predates the drum machines and synthesizers. *New school* is sometimes called fake music because it lacks real musicians and the creative flow that real musicians would allow.

new whips: 1) novice, inexperienced person. 2) new car.

nicca: see **nigga**.

nice: really good. "He was really *nice* on the mic."

nickel/nickle: 1) $5 bag of weed. 2) an attractive man.

nigga: nigger. Latin etymology is *necro*, which means dead. Metaphorically, perhaps, nigger is one dead in spirit. 1) Black person in a deragatory or oppressive sense (offensive). 2) lazy person. 3) a term of familiar address to people of all races. 4) term used loosely in conversation among some Blacks in a nonthreatening way as a reference to one another. Tupac redefined the term as an acronym to mean Never Ignorant Getting Goals Accomplished. Not all Black people are comfortable with using the term because of the history of the word, but taking a word that was used to hurt and redefining it works psychologically to soften the meaning or give it less impact. Much like how some women flip the word "bitch" in reference to themselves. As quoted by rapper Mos Def, nigger "displays the schizophrenic nature of the Black experience in America."

nigganet: network of Black people. "I heard about that through the *nigganet*."

nigga please: statement of disbelief.

nigga-rich: rich person with bad credit and irresponsible spending habits.

niggeritis: to feel sleepy after eating, also known as "the *itis*."

nina: nine-millimeter pistol.

nine: tech nine gun.

nino: gang boss. Name comes for the lead character in the Black crime film *New Jack City.*

nips: Asians (offensive).

N.O./Naw'lins: New Orleans, Louisiana.

no diggity: that's the truth, no doubt about it.

no half steppin': no procrastination.

NOI: Nation of Islam. A religious movement based on Black economic self-sufficiency led by Minister Louis Farrakhan.

'noids: marijuana-induced paranoia.

nookie: sex.

no sir: really? (MA)

Notorious B.I.G.: Christopher Wallace. Rapper. Called a natural-born lyricist and perhaps the best rapper who ever lived. Shot to death in Los Angeles March 9, 1997. B.I.G. stands for Business Instead of Games. A.k.a. Biggie, Big Poppa, Biggie Smalls.

nth degree: highest level.

nu: 1) Greek letter. 2) new. 3) Nubian/Black. "*Nu* Princess."

nuff' said: enough said.

number one with a bullet: rising fast.

nunya': none of your business.

nu rag: much like a do-rag but more appropriate for outdoor wear. Style created by street b-ball players who would take their T-shirts and wrap them around their heads and knot the end in a bun.

nut: 1) semen. 2) idiot.

nuts: 1) testicles. 2) crazy. 3) courage.

Nuyorican Poets Café: Lower East Side of Manhattan dive for poets, artists, and hip-hop heads to display their talent.

N.W.A.: Niggas With Attitude, rap group from California who led the scene in gangsta rap. Rap songs also filled with politics and social commentary and antiauthority messages.

O <<<

o: oochie—highly sexual girl.

Oaktown: Oakland, California.

O.E.: Old English malt liquor.

off the bat: immediately; doing something right away.

off the chain, off da' heezy fa' geezy, off the dome, off the meat rack, off the meter, off the wall: 1) good. 2) crazy.

off the cuff: spontaneous.

off the hook: 1) out of control. 2) fun.

off the titty: from the beginning.

off the wanger: good. (WI)

OG: old gangster/original gangster. Veteran gang member.

OJ: 1) orange juice. 2) Ford Bronco. The type of SUV O. J. Simpson drove while fleeing police after murder charges were brought against him for the death of his wife and a delivery man.

OKC: Oklahoma City, a.k.a. Tornado Alley.

okie-doke: 1) the runaround. 2) trickery, up to no good. 3) way of saying "okay."

old school/old skool: music or artists that predate drum machines and synthesizers. People refer to *old school* music as real music because there was the chance for new creations through live musicians.

old soul: person with knowledge beyond years of his/her age.

on a dime: in a moment's notice.

on fire: doing well.

on ice: incarcerated.

on lock: under control.

on point: correct. "He *on point* like Stacey Adams."

on swoll: 1) built up physically by weights. 2) puffed up mentally by success.

on the block: hustling.

on the come up: prospering.

on the low: low key, down low.

on the money: on target.

on the cover up: hiding something.

on the one: one turntable.

on the prowl: looking for something, mainly a sexual conquest.

on the real: truth.

on the strength: you have my word.

on (my) tip: liking a person and showing it.

one love: 1) unifying statement that was the mantra for a song. 2) salutation.

106 & Park: BET video show with Free and AJ as hosts.

187: police code for homicide.

one: a way of saying "good-bye," "peace."

one-liners: jokes.

one-mo-gen: again.

open: receptive. "That beat had everyone wide *open*."

O.P.P. 1) other people's pussy. **2)** other people's property. **3)** Ontario Provincial Police.

Oreo: Black person who tries to act white. Black on outside, white on inside, like the Oreo cookie.

outlaw: hard-core gangsta rapper.

Outrageous Flavors: ice cream parlor in New Jersey founded by The Outsidaz rap group. The store features hip-hop flavors like Rah Diggas "Imperial Chocolate," Outsidaz "Chocolate Chip U Up," Eminem's "Vanilla No Ice."

out the box: 1) fresh, exciting. **2)** good.

out the cage: good.

out the gate: to begin with.

out there: strange.

ovah: 1) good. **2)** end.

over my head: to misunderstand.

overstand: to understand, be clear on an issue.

packin': 1) to carry a gun. 2) endowed male.

pad: residence.

paid/paid in full: rich.

palms up: push palms upward in a gesture to raise the roof to demonstrate having a good time.

pana: term of familiar address.

pancakes: pills, prescription or nonprescription.

P&D: pressing (manufacturing) and distributing.

paper: money.

paper-chaser: one seeking money.

paperwork gangster: legal hustle.

pappi: daddy.

Parappa the rapper 2: rapper on Sony PlayStation 2.

Park Ave. babe/chick: rich, high-society girl.

parlay: 1) hangout. 2) transfer.

partner in rhyme: rap partner, i.e., Redman and Method Man.

party starter: see **hype-man**.

pass: 1) allowing members of one gang to go into the territory of another gang without harm. (CA) 2) allowing someone to get away with saying something stupid without dissing them back.

passion mark: mark created from sucking on body during intimacy; hickey.

pa'tna: partner.

patois: a dialect.

pattin' pies: having sex.

pay the piper: endure consequences.

payola: giving favor for money, i.e., a DJ playing a record because a record company paid him to play it. It is, at least, unethical and, at most, illegal.

PD: program director for radio. The person responsible for deciding which songs will be played.

P.E.: Public Enemy. Rap group. Original members Chuck D (Carlton Ridenhour), DJ Terminator X (Norman Rogers), Professor Griff (Richard Griffin), Flava Flav (William Drayton). Politically conscious and militant rap group who brought politics to hip-hop.

peace: a greeting, salutation.

peace out: said upon departure, "good-bye."

peach: pretty girl. (DS)

peaches: 1) pretty girls. 2) New Orleans record store. 3) breasts.

peasy: nappy hair, especially short and curly in the back.

peckerwood: white person (offensive).

peel a cap: fire a weapon.

peep (this): look at this.

peeps: people, friends or family.

pen: jail.

pencil pushers: journalists.

period: menstruation.

perkin' music: house music—up-tempo dance music. (WI)

perp/perpin': perpetrating, pretending.

perving: behaving in sexually suggestive manner.

pesos: money.

P-Funk: Parliament Funkadelics. Funk group famous for its futuristic instrumentation and creative lyrics.

Phat: attractive.

Phat Farm: hip-hop clothing line created by Russell Simmons.

P.H.D.: player-hating degree. Title awarded to a jealous person.

phone bone: phone sex.

phone off the hook: police are coming.

phyne: especially attractive man or woman, emphasis on "phy."

pie: vagina.

piece: 1) gun. 2) penis. 3) location. "It was wild up in that *piece*." 4) girl. 5) art (graffiti).

pigeon: irresponsible female who pretends to have more than she really does.

pigs: police.

pimp: to take advantage or misuse someone.

pimp daddy: a person whose style evokes thoughts of the small-time urban hustler.

pimped out: stylishly dressed.

pimp-hop: rap that talks about pimping and features videos with '70s perms, flare-leg pants, and hookers.

pinky ring: symbol of power for leader or person in charge, à la *The Godfather*, kiss the ring.

pipe: 1) penis. 2) sex. 3) crack pipe.

pipe dreams: wish, hope.

Pinoy: Filipino American.

pipes: great singing voice.

pissed (off): angry.

PJs: projects—urban housing developments for the poor.

plait: braid.

plates: cars, as in license plates.

platinum: a record that has sold one million copies.

platinum respect: highest regard in the music industry.

play: 1) trick or fool. 2) attention. "She's getting big *play* with that tight-ass dress on." 3) the slapping of hands as a form of greeting or salutation.

playa'/player: 1) person with multiple partners. 2) one who can get a girl/guy to do what he/she wants him/her to do.

played/played out: has been.

player hater: jealous person.

play high post: act snobby.

please believe!: statement of fact.

plucked: crazy.

plugged in: included.

PMS'ng: unnecessary attitude of a mean woman.

PNB: Post No Bills. A hip-hop clothing line. Company name comes from the construction site signs that read "POST NO BILLS." To paraphrase the label meaning, it means don't front.

P-noid: 1) paranoid. 2) upset or angry.

P.O.: 1) police officer. 2) probation officer.

pockets: having lots of money. "He got some deep *pockets*."

pockets like rabbit ears: Lots of money, long like rabbit ears.

pockets on E: out of money.

poem: lyrics.

poet: rapper.

poetrusic: combination of the two terms poetry and music.

poetry hustlers: rappers.

points: 1) credit for action. "Although his album fell flat he get *points* for trying." 2) Music industry term that defines how an artist will be paid. Retail royalties for an artist usually run 11–18 points; one point is roughly eight cents per unit sold in retail royalties.

poli: politics.

politicking: playing games. Peep the way the word is spelled. The "ticking" part means time is running out to make a political difference.

politricks: American politics gone awry. "President Clinton was up to some *politricks* when he said, 'It depends on what the meaning of is is.'"

pony: penis.

pootie-tang: sex.

pop: 1) to shoot. 2) to hit.

pop-lockin': a break dance.

po'-po: police.

popped off: occurred.

poppin': 1) a break dance. 2) happening scene. "This place is *poppin'* tonight."

poppin' trunks: tailgating.

pop that pussy: 1) dance hard and sexy. 2) have wild sex.

pork chops: police.

posse'/possie: group of hanging buddies.

postal: crazy.

posted: drunk.

pot: marijuana.

pound: 1) fist-to-fist greeting. 2) basketball court.

powder: 1) passive person. 2) cocaine.

powerhouse: 1) highly accomplished person. 2) person of great talent.

power-pill: good song.

pre-rappers: people like Gil Scott Heron and The Last Poets, who were speaking urban poetry in song before the advent of rap.

press: 1) manufacture CDs. 2) persistent behavior. "He kept *pressing* her about the promotion," (see **press up**).

pressed: concerned. "I ain't *pressed*."

press up: on someone's back. "She keeps *pressing me up* for cash."

prima dogs: the male version of a prima donna.

primer: lesson.

primo: marijuana cigarette mixed with crack cocaine.

Prince Paul: Paul Houston. Producer. Credited with creating the hip-hop album by layering it with cohesive themes.

private parts: sexual anatomy.

pro: 1) prostitute. 2) professional.

profilin': posturing.

projects: low-income housing, government-assisted living (see **PJs**).

props: credit, kudos, respect.

pros: girls.

pseudo thug: thug posturing.

PSL's: pussy-sucking lips.

PS2: PlayStation 2. Sony remote video game.

Public Enemy: see **P.E.**

Puff Daddy: Sean Combs. Rapper, producer, business executive: creator of Sean John clothing line and Justin's restaurant chain. Went from music intern to music industry mogul. Took commercial rap to new heights. A.k.a. P. Diddy, Puffy.

pull no punches: to tell the truth, tell it like it is.

pull trump card/ pull your card: to recognize the person behind façade.

pull up: to punch, fight.

pull your ho' card: to challenge the will of a person to see if he/she can stand up to his/her word.

pumpin': loud and effective. "That bass is *pumpin'*."

pump the brakes: watch your mouth.

punk: 1) passive person. 2) effeminate male.

punany: vagina.

puppy love: infatuation.

push-up: approach.

pussy: 1) passive person. 2) punk. 3) vagina.

pussy-whipped: female domination of a man. "That girl got him *pussy-whipped*."

put down: to support, back, or recommend. "I *put him down* with my company."

put it down: to act on something. "Toni Blackmon be *puttin' it down* on wax."

put your money where your mouth is: to bet, gamble. Put up or shut up.

PWT: poor white trash: 1) financially poor white person. 2) unsophisticated white person (offensive).

<<<

QB: Queensbridge, New York.

QP's: quarter pound of weed.

Q.T.: quiet tip. To speak with discretion. "Let's keep that on the *q.t.*"

Q-tip: Kamaal Fareed. Rapper. Former member of the Bohemian-style rap group A Tribe Called Quest. Coined the term "vivrant." A.k.a. Abstract Poet, Jonathan Davis.

Quad City: Orlando, Florida.

Queen Bee: see **Lil' Kim.**

Queen Latifah: Dana Owens. Rapper, actor, talk-show host, music executive. One of the first ladies to go mainstream in hip-hop. She rapped hard-core and went head to head with her male counterparts but made her mark using Afrocentric imagery and language that elevated the status of women. Was a star on the hip-hop television show *Living Single*.

Queensbridge projects: government-assisted housing in Queensbridge, New York. The largest housing project in the USA.

Quiet storm: something big about to happen that no one is expecting. "I hear Bad-boy got a *quiet storm* brewing in his camp."

quovadis: a low haircut that's even all over.

radar: standout. "She's *radar*."

radio-ready: rap songs with cuss words bleeped.

rag/raggin': 1) clothes. 2) a nicely dressed person. 3) to tease. "They were *raggin'* him about his haircut." 4) menstruation.

ragamuffin music: cuss-free, nonviolent lyrics.

ragamuffin: unkempt man or woman.

rain closet: shower.

raise up: leave.

Rakim: William Griffin. Rapper. Credited with modernizing rap with his conversational flow.

rally: term of familiar address, like homey. "That's my *rally*." (TX)

rap: 1) a verbal sport—word play competition. 2) tell a story or offer a message through rhymed lyrics, usually over music. 3) talk to in an intimate way in an effort to know someone better. "Come here girl, let me *rap* to you about something." 4) an acronym: rhythym-aggressive poetry.

Rap City: rap video show on BET cable network.

Rap Coalition: organization serving rappers and the rap music industry run by Wendy Day.

rap hustlin': making music to make money.

rap-lete: athlete who raps.

rapper: media-created, or at least media-driven, term to describe urban poet/lyricist.

rap-rock: the combining of rap and rock music in which head-banging bass and guitar blend with hip-hop lyrics.

Rapsheet: rap industry newspaper.

Rap Snacks: a brand of potato chips that features hip-hop artists on the bags.

rapspeak: the language of hip-hop.

raptor: a rapper-actor.

rap'zines: rap magazines.

Rastafari: a spiritual lifestyle in which practitioners adhere to a natural way of living, including smoking marijuana, which they view as a holy herb for spiritual enlightenment. The name is derived from the Black Ethiopian King (circa 1930) Ras Tafari Makonnen. A.k.a. Haile Selassie I. Followers regard Selassie as Jesus Christ incarnate.

Rastafarian: one who follows and practices Rastafari. Rasta man.

rat: tell.

raw: unadulterated.

raw dog: without a condom. "Some girls be wantin the jimmy *raw dog*." A.k.a. "bareback."

read: to set straight, correct, tell off.

read the hand/palm: a hand gesture where the palm of the hand is put in the direction of someone's face. It means "Stop talking to me."

recognize: respect.

Redman: Reggie Nobles. Rapper. Famous for his tag team raps with Method Man. A.k.a. Doc, Funk Dr. Spot.

red rum: code word for murder. "Murder" spelled backward, made popular in *The Shining*.

red velvet: blood from shoot-out or murder. "It was *red velvet* in the place after the shooting started."

reefer: marijuana.

reformed pigeon: woman reformed of her irresponsible ways.

reggie: right-hand turn in a vehicle.

remember where you come from: warning or advice to a person who has succeeded in leaving the ghetto from those left behind: don't let ego be your guide.

renegade: good rapper.

rep: represent, to be accounted for.

reparations: compensation for ill treatment by one group toward another. African Americans are fighting for reparations for the enslavement of their ancestors.

retro: when the old is new again.

re-up: renew.

rewire: re-create previously recorded music.

RIAA: Recording Industry Association of America. It is a trade association for the creation and distribution of music in the U.S. The organization keeps track of U.S. record sales.

ride: car. "That my *ride* over there, the 'Lac."

ride or die: a commitment that requires a decision. To ride is someone who will be there for the long haul. Or die is someone who will bail out when the going gets tough. "I need a *ride or die* chick."

ride the beat: to bounce with a beat as if the music is driving the body instead of your own blood.

right chea': right here. "The man *right chea'*!"

right-on: correct.

Rikers Island: prison in Upstate NY.

rilla': real, truth.

rim/rim job: anal oral sex.

rims: fancy hubcaps for a car.

R.I.P.: rest in peace.

rip: 1) perform especially well. "He *ripped* the mic." 2) steal. "She *ripped* him off big time."

rip-hop: stolen lyrics. Lyrics ripped off from another song.

ripped: 1) chiseled body. 2) to set straight on an issue. 3) to beat in competition.

River City: Memphis, Tennessee.

rizzi: transportation (see **ride**).

roach: 1) deceptive person. 2) the end of a marijuana cigarette.

road dog: travel partner, hanging buddy.

roadie an artist's tour assistant.

Roaster: Ferrari.

rob the cradle: to have sex with a significantly younger person.

Roc-A-Wear: hip-hop clothing.

rock: 1) to wear, as in clothing. 2) crack cocaine. 3) a basketball. 4) a diamond. 5) to do something well. 6) to have sex. 7) a dance in which the body swings back and forth.

rocket: drug, anything that gets one high.

rock star: crack addict.

rock the cradle: kill.

Rockwilder: 1) Rottweiler, a breed of dog developed in Germany. 2) dope music producer.

Rolie/Roly: Rolex timepiece.

roll/rollin': 1) laughing. 2) selling drugs. 3) on a positive roll—doing well. 4) fight. "They *rolled* on him for making racist comments." 5) leave. 6) successful or having lots of money.

rollers: police. (MI)

rollies: rolling paper for tobacco or marijuana.

Rolling Stone: 1) male with children all over the place. 2) music magazine.

roll on: 1) to have a good time. 2) to fight.

Rollo: guy with no fashion sense, derived from the badly dressed male character from the hit TV sitcom *Good Times*.

roll 'o: good-bye.

roll up: to go to someone's location with the express purpose of beating them up.

roots: feet.

Roots, Rhymes, and Rage: The Hip-Hop Story: an exhibit at the Rock and Roll Hall of Fame in Cleveland, Ohio.

Rosco: gun. "He got *Rosco* with him."

rotors: good voice.

Rotten Apple: Harlem, New York.

rough-neck: roguish male; thug.

'round the way girl: girl from the neighborhood.

rubber: condom

Rucker Park: famous outdoor basketball court in Harlem, New York.

rudy-poo: slacker.

ruffians: rowdy group.

rump shaker: music that makes you want to dance or shake your rump; good-sounding music.

rump: butt.

run: to cost. "How much will that *run* me?"; also a directive to someone about to be robbed: "*Run* your jacket" or "*Run* your sneakers."

run amuck: out of control.

Run-D.M.C.: Rap group. Run (Joseph Simmons, reverend and brother of rap industry mogul Russell Simmons), DMC (Darryl McDaniels), DJ Jam Master Jay (Jason Mizell). The trio brought rap to the mainstream. Inspired many to rap. Took hip-hop sound international. Five gold and platinum rap albums.

run for the money: create competition.

running crew: hanging buddies.

running man: a dance made popular in the early 1990s in music videos; it's like using a Stairmaster exercise machine but you're on a dance floor.

runs: diarrhea. Liquid waste that forces one to run as opposed to walk to the bathroom or else . . .

Russell Simmons: Music executive, entrepreneur. Among the first to capitalize on hip-hop culture. The force behind Def Jam Records, one of the first hip-hop record labels. Simmons created Phat Farm and Baby Phat urban clothing lines and Rush Communications. Called the "Godfather of Rap." Credited with taking rap mainstream. A socially conscious businessman, among the ranks of men like Muhammad Ali, who acts with political, historical, and social responsibility to his community.

S <<<

sack(s): 1) money. 2) bag of drugs.

sack chaser: person seeking money.

Sac-Town: Sacramento, California.

sag: fashion.

Salt-N-Pepa: Salt (Cheryl James), Pepa (Sandra Denton). Female rap group. The first female rap group to sell more than one million records. They rapped lyrics of female empowerment, self-reliance, and self-respect. Their DJ is Spinderella (Dee Dee Roper).

samiches: sandwiches.

sample: to use pieces of other recorded music in the creation of new or updated music.

sand toward the bottom of the hour glass: fat butt.

scanky: sleazy.

scattered, smothered, and covered: Southern-style hash browns made at the Waffle House restaurant. (DS)

school: to teach the lessons of life.

science: 1) knowledge. 2) lesson. "KRS one be droppin' mad *science* in his tracks."

Scooby-Doo: marijuana rolled in cigar paper after tobacco has been dumped from its casing (see **blunt**).

scoop(ed): 1) latest information or gossip. 2) to be the first.

scrap: fight.

scratch: 1) money. 2) a music art form (see **scratch music**).

scratch music: a rhythmic sound made from sliding a turntable needle back and forth on top of a vinyl record. Technique created by Grand Wizard Theodore.

scrazy: the combination of the two terms "scary" and "crazy."

screw-face: frown.

scribes: writers/rappers.

scrilla: money.

scrubs: irresponsible men; basketball players with weak games and big mouths.

seafood lover: a person who likes performing oral sex on a woman.

Sean John: hip-hop clothing line created by Sean John "P. Diddy" Combs.

see: understand. "You *see* what I'm sayin?"

seeds: children.

seen: beat up.

sellin' like hotcakes: selling fast.

sell-out/sold-out: 1) person who betrays the loyalty of another for personal gain. 2) to sell all tickets for an event.

semi: marijuana cigarette.

send it up: to challenge to fight or do battle.

sensimilla: a type of marijuana. A.k.a. sensi.

sent up north: sent to jail.

serve: give.

serve up: go to battle, physical or verbal, on an issue. Tell off.

sessed (out): high on marijuana.

set: 1) crew, group. 2) gathering. "I'm having a *set* at my place tonight, you should stop by." 3) streets or neighborhood.

set it off: start. "We 'bout to *set it off* up in here."

set-trippin': division among the group.

730: crazy.

sewed up: in control of a situation.

sex pockets: drugs, like ecstasy, said to induce wet dreams.

shade: deliberate disrespect. "She was giving him *shade* at the party." Also, underhanded or untrustworthy.

Shady: covertly disrespectful.

shakedown: police bust.

shank: 1) refers to a knife. 2) to cut. "I'm gone *shank* his ass if he don't give me my money."

Shaolin/The Rock: Staten Island, New York.

Shaolin slang: language of the Wu-Tang Clan; Staten Island slang.

sharp: 1) nicely dressed. 2) intelligent. 3) biting language. "She has a *sharp* tongue." 4) good.

shell corp: a dummy corporation that only exists on paper.

Shell-toe Adidas: sport shoes designed by Adidas that have a shell pattern on the front in the toe area. Run-DMC made the shoes famous.

sherm: sherman cigar soaked in embalming fluid. (CA)

shero: the female version of hero.

shield: condom.

shift: sell.

shift-bricks: sell records.

shine: standout.

shine the skin: oral sex.

shit: reference to something, anything, good or bad. "That song is the *shit.*"

shit bricks: terrified.

shit on: 1) betray (see **brown showers**).

shit-talkin': 1) bragging. 2) nonsense.

shiz-nits: good. "That's the *shiz-nits.*"

shock value: an action to get a reaction.

shoida than show: surer than sure.

sho-nuff: surely enough.

shook: scared.

shoot-a-kite: mail a letter.

shooting up: intravenous drug use.

shoot joints: throw punches.

short on: lacking. "He's *short on* cells." "I'm *short on* cash."

shorty/shawty: 1) attractive person. 2) term of familiar address that can refer to either gender. (DS)

shot caller: leader, person in charge.

shot down: denied.

shotgun: front passenger seat of a car. "I got *shotgun*." Also, a way for two people to share a strong hit of marijuana.

shot to the mouth: punch in the face.

shouts/shout out: recognition.

showing off: exhibiting behavior that begs for attention.

showtime: start.

shut-eye: sleep.

shut-up: statement of disbelief, like "Say it ain't so."

sick/sickening: 1) unbelievable. 2) good. "That beat is *sickening*."

sike (psyche): to play mind games; trick or fool.

singin': stinky, smelly.

Sing-Sing: New York prison.

'Sip: Mississippi.

Six: Mercedes six hundred series.

6 feet deep: dead.

six-pack: well-toned abdominal muscles.

6-shooter: gun.

skank: lascivious female.

skate: person who tries to get by in the easiest way.

skeelo: plan. "What's the *skeelo*?"

skeeze/skeezer/skeeza: woman who is known for sleeping with a lot of men; an easy lay.

skelly: children's street game, in which the court is drawn on the ground in chalk and played with bottle caps.

skid-bid: jail time.

skills: talent.

skinny: latest happening on information, details.

skins: 1) condoms. 2) money. 3) marijuana wrapping paper.

skippy: agreeable. "You damn *skippy*."

ski-trip: to use cocaine.

skitzing: acting crazy.

skully: skull cap.

skunk: marijuana.

skurred: scared.

slab: 1) street/expressway. (TN) 2) dead body.

slam: 1) a dance where people slam bodies against one another. 2) a hip-hop movie.

slammin': 1) having sex. 2) a good time. "That party was *slammin'*."

slang doc (tor): person who has mastered the use of slang and who creates new slang.

slang game: rap; toying with words.

slangin' iron: firing or brandishing a gun.

slang therapist: rap artist.

slanguage: the combination of the two terms "slang" and "language."

slap-sessions: 1) music-making sessions where the first person who falls asleep gets slapped. 2) sexual intercourse.

slavery: forced servitude; ownership of one human being by another.

slayed: sexed.

slay me: you make me laugh.

sleeper: boredom.

slept: missed out on.

slice it up: have sex.

sling: sell.

slizzard: whorish female.

sloppy seconds: a person you sex after a friend already has had him/her.

slow jam: ballad.

slow motion: slow moving; state of existence that means not much is happening. "Things are *slow motion* around here."

slow your role: slow down. (DS)

spot: 1) happening place. 2) to loan. "*Spot* me ten bucks 'til I get my paycheck next week." (See **G spot**.)

slug: gold tooth/teeth. (DS)

slugged up: mouth with multiple gold teeth. (DS)

slummin': hanging out, relaxing.

smack: crack cocaine; heroin.

smacked up: pregnant.

smack-talking/talking smack: 1) telling lies. 2) verbal insults.

smell me: see **feed me**.

smelling beans: broke, no money.

smoke: 1) cigarettes. 2) marijuana.

smoked: 1) shot. 2) killed.

smoked out: 1) high on drugs. 2) shot at.

snake: 1) evil person. 2) dance move in which one wriggles like a snake.

snaky: underhanded activity.

snap: 1) to put someone in check, reprimand. 2) epiphany, to understand something, like a light turned on. "Oh, *snap*." 3) gesture where one literally snaps a finger after a statement to emphasize a point, like the period at the end of a sentence.

snap ya neck: nod your head to the beat.

snatch: vagina.

sneakers: sport shoes (see **gym shoes**).

Snoop Dogg: Calvin Broadus. Rapper. Laid-back, soothing flow in his sound and lyrics. Rapper who makes the creation of the art seem effortless.

snow: 1) cocaine. 2) white person.

snow bunny: white female.

snowed: tricked/fooled.

soft: 1) meek or mild-mannered person. 2) clean lyrics. "He be rocking some *soft* lyrics."

soul patch: goatee.

S.O.L.: shit out of luck.

soldier/soulja: loyal friend, comrade.

some: sex. "You gona gimme *some* tonight?"

son: term of familiar address, usually toward a younger male, not necessarily the offspring. Also a term of endearment among friends who are not related.

sophomore jinx: when second album fails to do as well as the first.

sorry: lazy. "She left his *sorry* ass because he wasn't even trying to pay his bills."

SOS: smash on site—fight.

soulja rags: bandanas. (DS)

Soulquarians: network of arty or more creative forces in hip-hop who are passionate about their work and the perseverance of the hip-hop culture. When the group started, many of them happened to be Aquarians.

sound bomb: good music.

sounding off: 1) stinking, malodorous. 2) venting.

sound providers: speakers.

soundscan: organization that tabulates record sales.

Southern soul hip-hop: rap that speaks of the Southern experience.

Space City: Houston, Texas.

Spanglish: combination of the two terms "Spanish" and "English" (attributed to Puerto Ricans).

spark: to light. "*Spark* a j."

speaker staples: records in heavy rotation.

speed: a drug, like crystal meth, that can be used as an upper or downer.

speed-knot: bump on the head caused by a blow. "When the cops arrested him, he caught a *speed-knot* from a knight stick."

Spic: a Spanish-speaking person (offensive).

spin doctors: deejays.

spin master: DJ.

spins: radio airplay. Each time a record is played, it's considered a spin.

spirits: alcohol.

spit: 1) to rap. 2) to brag. "He *spitting* about his new ho'."

spit fire: to rap well.

spliff: marijuana rolled into a cigarette.

sport: to wear; to show off new clothing.

spot: a place to hang out.

spray: 1) to shoot into a crowd. 2) to contribute to a song as a guest artist.

sprung: 1) obsessed; the willingness to do anything for a mate. 2) to be released from jail.

squar: single cigar sold out of the box. (FL)

square biz: square business, serious business.

square: 1) really? 2) boring person or person who doesn't take risks.

squeezed off: pulled the trigger of a gun.

squo (w): 1) squo means Square, as in "square business" or serious business. 2) a hip-hop clothing label.

stable: home.

Stacey Adams: designer, especially known for pointy-toe shoes.

stack money/paper/bones: to earn, make, or save money.

St. Andrews Hall: three-story dance club. Called the best place in the world to find mainstream and pure underground hip-hop. Located in Detroit, Michigan.

stank: rude behavior.

stankin': good. "That beat is *stankin'*."

Stapleton projects: government-assisted housing in Staten Island.

steal/stole: to hit or sneak in a punch while fighting.

steelo/steez: 1) confidence, attitude, drive. 2) style. 3) the happening. "What's the *steelo?*"

step to me: a challenge to physically fight or do battle.

sticks: see **ghetto**.

stick-up kid/kings: thief/thieves.

stiff: 1) to kill. 2) dead (body). 3) to take advantage of.

stogie: surgically enhanced cigar, split, dumped of its tobacco, and filled with marijuana.

stoked: excited.

stomp: to wear. "He *stomping* some sharp shoes." (DS)

stompin' grounds: home or hangout area.

stone cold: mean, stoic, without feeling.

stop the madness: stop acting crazy.

storyteller: rapper.

straight no chaser: straightforward and honest.

straight up: in truth.

strap: to carry a weapon. "When the police caught her, she was *strapped.*"

strawberry: woman who sells sex for drugs.

strawberry fruitgazee: flamboyant male homosexual.

street: 1) inner-city life and living. 2) unsophisticated behavior.

street-bred: raised in the streets.

street buzz: gossip and rumors.

street heat: 1) stylish hip-hop clothing. 2) unregistered gun.

street marketing: 1) hustling. 2) culture-based marketing.

street pharmacist: drug dealer.

street poets: rappers or lyricists whose words don't fit into traditional categories.

street scarf: bandana.

street style: adapting to the behavior of the inner-city environment.

stretches: years of a person's prison term.

strikes: years, usually number of years for prison term.

Strong Island: Long Island, New York.

stuck: high on ecstasy.

stuck on stupid: not getting the point.

stuck up: snobby.

student of life: person who learned from experience.

studio gangster: gangster on record but not in real life.

stunna: 1) rapper. 2) heavily laden with stunning jewelry. (DS)

stunt: 1) to steal. 2) offensive action.

stupid: intelligent.

stylin': fashionably dressed.

subs: magazine subscription.

Subterranean purist: lover of underground (nonmainstream) hip-hop, which is said to be hip-hop in its purist form. Promotes individuality and creativity; materialism is downplayed. A.k.a. subterranean underground.

subway: most prized canvas for graf artists.

subway entertainers: bandit of young bruhs who dance on the NYC subway for tips during transit rides.

sucker-punch: to punch somebody when they're not prepared to fight.

sucker MC: bad MC.

sugar daddy: the male provider in a relationship, usually in exchange for the relationship itself.

Sugar Hill Gang: rap group. Big Bank Hank (Henry Jackson), Master Gee (Guy O'Brien), Wonder Mike (Michael Wright). Made and sang the first major hip-hop song, "Rappers Delight," in October 1979. Took hip-hop sound nationwide.

sugar in the tank: suspected of male homosexuality.

sugar-water: sugar and water mix poor people use when they don't have milk for cereal.

suit: businessman.

sumpin, sumpin: something, reference to any object or thing but usually refers to sex.

sunkiss: heroin.

sunny: good.

Super-dupa-fly: superfly to a higher power.

superfly: cool cat with a hip style of dress; a ladies' man.

sushi: Asian person (offensive).

suspect: suspicious person. Could also refer to sexually suspicious person, i.e., homosexual. "He *suspect*, so watch out for him."

SUV: sports utility vehicle.

swag: walk.

swangin': good. "That beat is *swangin'*."

SWAT: Southwest, Atlanta.

sweat: to hotly pursue.

sweat box: small club.

sweet: 1) appealing, nice. "That's a *sweet* ride you got." 2) to like someone. "He *sweet* on you, girl." 3) effeminate male.

swerve: enjoyment; groove. "Getting your *swerve* on."

swing: chain. "Nelly is rocking a platinum *swing* with the number one on it."

swisha: a cigar dumped of its contents and used as rolling paper for marijuana. (TX)

swisha mixes: mixing music while high on drugs. (TX)

switch hitter: bisexual.

swoll: 1) puffed up physically by weights. 2) puffed up mentally by success.

sword swallower: person who performs oral sex on a man.

scribe: writer.

syrup: cough medicine mixed with codeine and prometh.

<<<

t: scoop, gossip.

tack head: tacky person.

T.A.F.K.A.: an acronym used for the Minnesota singer/rapper Prince, which means The Artist Formerly Known As. He has since changed his name back to Prince. Prolific writer. Held number-one spot for a movie and song at the same time with *Purple Rain*.

tag: 1) physically hit. 2) the signature of a graffiti artist. 3) to write (graf) on something. 4) sex.

take for broke: to take advantage of.

take it to the bridge: to maximize one's effort.

take it to the head: to maximize a situation.

take no prisoners: to make sure everyone is involved.

Taki 183: one of the first graffiti artists on the scene with works that date back to the 1960s.

tales from the 'hood: stories from the ghetto.

talkin' trash/shit: 1) bragging. 2) telling lies.

talking out cha' neck: see **talkin' trash**.

talk to: an attempt to establish an intimate relationship. "He's still trying to *talk to* that girl. She ain't interested in him."

talk to the hand: a hand gesture where the palm of the hand is put in the direction of someone's face. It means, "Stop talking to me."

tall drink o' water: attractive tall person.

T&A: titties and ass.

tank: 1) vagina. 2) voluptuous female body. 3) failure.

tap: 1) sex. "I'm gone *tap* dat ass tonight." 2) fight.

tat: tattoo.

tax: 1) to rob. 2) to drain. "That new album *taxed* me, dog." 3) cost.

teabaggin': oral sex on testicles, man is in position with testicles hanging in person's mouth.

tear off: give money.

teaser: the first released song from an upcoming album.

tec: tech-nine weapon.

Tec-one: spy shop in Brooklyn, NY.

Teflon: nothing sticks, namely criminal charges.

tell/told off: to set straight, make clear.

telly: television.

tender/tenderoni: pretty girl.

ten mil: ten million sales of one record (see **diamond**).

Temple of Hip-hop: hip-hop preservation society created by KRS One.

tetas: breasts.

thang: thing.

that freaked me out: surprised.

that's the move: that's the thing to do, the appropriate action to take. (The opposite would be "that ain't the move"—the inappropriate thing to do.)

The Bassment: BET rap video show hosted by Big Tigger. Tigger also hosts the morning radio show on WJLB in Detroit.

The Big Easy: New Orleans.

The Big River: Mississippi.

the bomb: very good.

The Box: call-in video request show on the cable network.

the breaks: stroke of bad luck.

The Burghs: Pittsburgh, Pennsylvania.

The D: Detroit, Michigan.

The Desert: Queens, New York.

The Five Points: the five boroughs of NYC: Queens, Manhattan, Staten Island, Bronx, Brooklyn.

the game: life/thug life.

The Ice Opinion: *Pimptionary,* created by Ice-T.

The Igloo: Minneapolis, Minnesota.

the "man": 1) white man, the oppressor. 2) bossy Black man. 3) successful male.

the other side of midnight: A.M. hours.

the rage: the latest happening or in-style thing.

the real deal: something or someone of knockout caliber. Consider boxer Evander Holyfield whose moniker is "The Real Deal."

the "Real McCoy": the real thing.

The Rock: 1) Long Island, New York. 2) wrestler on the WWF, Duane Johnson.

the roof is on fire: party chant sang to the beat of the music: "The roof, the roof, the roof is on fire, we don't need no water let the motherfucker burn, burn motherfucker, burn!"

The Roots: Bohemian-style rap group who follow the old school tradition of playing instruments live.

the shit: good.

The Source: first published hip-hop magazine, 1988.

the stuff: can refer to anything good. "BG's new bay Hakim is *the stuff*."

the usual suspect: the Black male.

The Wood: Inglewood, California.

Third Coast: Southern-style rap.

third eye: intuition or sense of knowing.

thirty-eight/three-eight: .38 caliber pistol.

threads: 1) clothes. 2) piece of something, part in something.

three: bisexual, third sex.

304: whore. Term derived from beeper code read upside down to read hoe (whore).

through: 1) ugly. 2) end—fire, dismiss. "You're *through*!"

through thick n thin: promise/forever.

throw/threw-down: 1) fight/fought. 2) enjoy(ed). 3) to behave aggressively. 4) sex.

throw d'em bows: the elbow dance—hold your elbows in a boxing stance and alternately bump "bows" to the beat of the music with the person you're dancing with. (DS)

throwed: good. "Ya'll puttin out a hella *throwed* mag."

throw up: 1) vomit 2) graffiti.

throwing up the set: having a good time.

thug: petty criminal whose lawless acts primarily are to survive.

thugged-out: style of being, style of dress, i.e., hat to the back, which is the conditioning of the environment.

thug work out: to build muscle using what is available, like street light posts to do pull ups.

thumpin': 1) good sounding. 2) fighting.

tical: marijuana.

ticked off: angry, upset.

tics: girls.

tight: 1) outstanding. 2) close relationship. 3) good. "That beat is *tight*." 4) describes a woman's vagina.

Timbaland: Tim Mosley. Producer. He's called the beat wizard for making innovative sounds that changed the music of hip-hop. He calls it a "bassment" sound.

timbs: Timberland shoes.

time of the month: 1) period of mood swings for a man or woman. 2) menstruation.

Times Square: fun, exciting.

tina: see **crystal methamphetamine.**

tip: 1) penis. 2) snitch. 3) to like. "She's on my *tip*." (See **sweat**.)

tired: outdated.

titties: breasts.

TMI: too much information.

toast: ridicule in jest.

to a tee: exactly.

to boot: also.

to die for: a compliment filled with desire. "That suit is *to die for*."

toe jam: 1) party spot in LBC. (CA) 2) dirt between toes.

to' up from the flo' up: a person who is out of sorts from head to toe. (LBC)

To Maluco: I'm out of my mind. It is said when something is very good. (Brazil)

tomb: 1) jail. 2) grave.

tool: person being used by another.

too many things: a lot at one time, perhaps too much to handle at once. "He was *too many things*, I had to get rid of him."

tootsie roll: butt.

top dog: best.

Top Dog/Underdog: Broadway play featuring Mos Def (Dante Smith), the first rapper to star in a Broadway play. The play is about two fending bruhs from the ghetto. It was written by Suzan-Lori Parks and won the Pulitzer.

top-gunner: lead rapper in a group.

tore out the frame: 1) exhausted. 2) insulted.

Tornado Alley: Oklahoma City, Oklahoma.

toss salad: oral anal sex (first became popular because of Home Box Office documentary on prison system).

tow down: drunk.

toy cop: security guard; if they are armed, they only have a knight-stick.

toys: 1) material possessions. 2) to wipe or blot out the graffiti of another.

track: record.

track masters: producers.

track star: coward.

track-worker: 1) record producer. 2) drug dealer.

trade: bisexual male.

trap/trappings: 1) riches. 2) vagina.

trees: marijuana.

trick: 1) to sell sex. 2) prostitute.

tricked out: used up sexually; usually in reference to a girl who has had a lot of sex. "Don't fuck with her, man, that bitch is *tricked out*."

tricknology: mind games.

tricks of the trade: detailed lessons.

trife (trifling): whack, also lazy.

tril: excellent. "UGK been *tril* out the gate." (TX)

trim: vagina.

trip-hop: hip-hop with slow, manic grooves.

Triple 5 Soul: hip-hop sportswear.

Triple x: Amsterdam, Netherlands.

trippin': 1) having a good time. 2) someone who acts out of character. 3) weird behavior from doing drugs.

TRL: MTV show with Carson Daly as host.

trooper: 1) hard worker. 2) fan or other supporter.

truck: heavily laden with jewelry. "That mofo is *truck*."

true: honest, genuine, without pretense.

true 'dat (true that): I agree/affirmation.

trump: win.

trump tight: put together well, a winning hand. Consider the card game of Spades, where the trump is the winning card.

trunk: 1) butt. 2) energy. "That album got plenty of *trunk* in it."

trunk scan: to sell out of the trunk of a car.

trunk-thumping: heavy bass beat.

'tude: see **attitude**.

tunes: music.

Tunnel: New York nightclub famed for featuring hip-hop old school, new school, and the newest music to its crowd. Sunday nights Funkmaster Flex spins.

tunnel-banger: record that excites a crowd and sends them to the dance floor.

Tupac Shakur: controversial rap star known for his political, spiritual and heartfelt messages in his writing. Shot to death September 13, 1996. A.k.a. Makaveli, Pac, 2Pac. Lesane Parish Crooks was his birthname. His mom changed his name to Tupac Amuru (shining serpent) Shakur (thankful to God). Tupac was first in a group called Strictly Dope. He got his start with Digital Underground. He was also part of The New African Panthers.

turbo: marijuana.

turncoat: disloyal behavior.

turned out: no self-control. "She got *turned out* by her man, then by that crack."

turn it out: words of encouragement to do well. After having done well, one can brag and say, "I *turned it out*."

turntable technique: the art of the deejay.

turntablism: the art of deejaying.

turntablist: one who uses turntables as an instrument to create new rhythmic sounds.

Twista: Carl T. Mitchell, fastest rapper on the planet, according to *The Guinness Book of World Records 1992*.

twisted: 1) drunk. 2) wrong. "Don't get it *twisted*."

two comma kid: person with millions of dollars.

2way: two-way pager. A pager that allows you to send and receive messages.

Twurk: strip-dance. (DS)

U <<<

u-ey: u-turn in a vehicle. "Bust a *u-ey* right here—we're not driving in the right direction."

ugly: good or not good, depending on its usage. "That new beat is *ugly*."

Uncle L: see **L.L.Cool J**.

Uncle Sham: Uncle Sam.

Uncle Tom: Black man who wants to be white or who caters to white people.

underdig: understand.

underground: 1) nonmainstream music. 2) artists who are true to the hip-hop art form, despite whatever success.

underground battles: lyrical battles between MC's.

undie: underground.

unfucwitable: highly skilled; untouchable.

Universal Fat House: Hip-Hop church in Jersey City, New Jersey.

Universal Zulu Nation: long-standing international hip-hop music group started by hip-hop guru Afrika Bambaataa.

up north: jail.

up on it: aware.

ups: good basketball skills.

upstairs: 1) head. 2) heaven.

up the stakes: take to a higher level.

urban dwellers: people who live in the inner city.

urban soldier: fighter for justice.

Urrea: the area of and surrounding Washington, District of Columbia, the nation's capital.

Uzi: high-powered assault weapon.

V <<<

vamoose: disappear; beat it.

vapors: the feeling of being overwhelmed.

vatos: men.

veejay: video deejay.

verbal lashes: jokes, insults, or put-downs, usually by one opponent to another in an MC competition.

verbal mind food: socially conscious rap or rap with a message.

verbal rhyme phonies: putting words together that rhyme but don't always make clear sense.

Versace: high-fashion designer wear.

vest: bulletproof vest.

vexed: angry.

Vibe: 1) to connect. 2) a hip-hop magazine. 3) something emotive.

Vibeablicious: see **Vibe**.

vicked: robbed.

vinyl: album.

virtual cipher/cipher: online exchanges between hip-hop heads.

vivrant: impressive, uplifting.

VMB: video music box.

vogues: fancy car rims. "Rollin' *vogues*."

voulez vous couches avec moi: will you go to bed with me? (thanks to Patti LaBelle)

W <<<

wack/whack: 1) not good. 2) to hit or kill. "I *wacked* his ass."

wad: thick or large amount of anything.

wallflowers: those who stand against the wall at a party instead of being on the dancefloor.

walls: 1) vagina. 2) prison.

wally's: shoes by Clark Wallabee.

wannabe: pretender.

washed up: has-been.

wash dat' paper: turn illegal money clean by using it for good service.

wassup/whassup: what's up? A greeting.

waves: hairstyle achieved from continuous brushing.

wax: 1) beat up in a fight. 2) have sex. 3) record.

wax poetic: perform well lyrically.

wax reign: record on top of the play list.

wax slinger: deejay.

wax warriors: DJ's who battle in DJ competition.

waze out: syke. (CO)

WC: West Coast.

weave: human or synthetic hair braided or sewn into natural hair to give length or volume.

webeos: full-length, 3-D animated, interactive music videos.

wedgy: to have pants stuck between the butt cheeks.

weed: marijuana.

weight: drugs.

went down: 1) happened, occurred. 2) performed oral sex. 3) jail. (AL)

West Coast funk: soulful-sounding music under a variety of lyrical styles.

West Coast rap: traditionally known as gangster rap. Rap lyrics that detail sex, violence, and drugs, with slow, hypnotic grooves.

West Coast sway: a style of walk that has a sway. (CA)

wet: 1) sprayed with bullets. "Those gangsters *wet* the place." 2) shot. 3) sexually excited. 4) high on drugs.

wet behind the ears: young, inexperienced.

whalers: cry baby.

what!: an exclamation or a challenge, asking or suggesting, "Now what?"/"What can you say to this?"

what's da dillyo: what's the deal?

what's crackin': what's happening? (CA)

what's getting: what's happening?

what's poppin': what's going on?

what's the business: what's happening? (TN)

what time is it: rhetorical question to people to stand up and fight for their rights.

what up doe: yo, what's up?

wheels of steel: turntable.

whip: 1) good. "That new song is the *whip*." 2) nice car.

whipped: 1) nicely done. "Her hair is *whipped*." 2) exhausted. 3) see **pussy-whipped**.

whippersnap rap: beginner or elementary type rhymes, nothing new or innovative.

whips: 1) nightclubs. 2) cars.

whoa: 1) slow down. 2) a statement of surprise, like "wow." 3) impressive. 4) good.

whoadies: term of familiar address. (DS)

who-dee-who: catcall, usually directed at a girl or made when a pretty girl walks by. (DS)

whole-nine-yards/whole-shebang: the whole thing.

whore rap: rapper whose sole purpose is to get paid, no passion involved.

wicked: good.

wife-beaters: white cotton tank-top shirts that expose the arms. Prison inmates, made fashionable by hip-hop heads, wear the shirts. The name "wife-beater" is associated with big belly spousal abusers who always seem to be wearing one when they are arrested—see any episode of *Cops*.

wifey: girlfriend.

wig: 1) fake hair. 2) to behave radically.

wigger: white-nigger.

wiggin out: acting unusual.

wild thang: sex.

wildin' out: getting wild, acting crazy.

Will Smith: see **Fresh Prince**.

willies: feeling of repugnance.

windmills: a break dance.

with a quickness: right away.

wobble: stripper dance or dance females do that make their booties jiggle. (DS)

wolf-tickets: bluff, like the boy who cried wolf. "Don't pay any attention to him, he is always selling *wolf tickets*."

wood: 1) bad. 2) not selling well. "That album is *wood*, dawg." 3) exhausted. 4) penis.

woody: erect penis.

wooler blunts: marijuana mixed with crack cocaine.

woolers: crack cocaine.

woop de do: so what?

word/word up: 1) really? 2) to agree.

word is bond: you have my word.

wordsmith: rapper.

wordspray: rap.

work/work it: word of encouragement. "You better *work!*" Can describe any action.

World DJ Day: an annual event held each year in a different location to celebrate the art of the DJ.

worm: dance move in which one moves the body on the floor like a worm.

wreck: 1) fight. 2) recreation.

wrecking crew: 1) boast of rap groups who each say one can destroy or "wreck" the other lyrically. They call themselves "wrecking crews." 2) gang of violent thugs.

wrecking shop: winning an MC battle.

writer: grafitti artist.

writing checks yo' ass can't cash: bluffing about one's ability.

Wu-bonics: innovative language of the Wu-Tang Clan. The comingling of words that sound good but don't always make clear sense, i.e., using the name "lobster head" to make a rhyme.

Wu-juice: 40 ounces (of beer).

Wu-Tang Clan: nine member rap group out of Staten Island, New York, that changed the sound of East Coast hip-hop with masterful beats, colorful imagery, and the layering of kung-fu mythology. RZA (Robert Diggs), Genius/GZA (Gary Grice), Method Man (Clifford Smith),

Raekwon the Chef (Corey Woods), Ghostface Killah (Tony Stark/Dennis Coles), Ol' Dirty Bastard (Russell Jones), Rebel INS/Inspectah Deck (Jason Hunter), Capadonna (Darly Hill), Mastah Killah (Jamal Turner).

Wyclef Jean: Rapper, producer, who along with his group The Fugees took rap to global heights addressing and expressing international concerns. A.k.a. Nelly Nell.

X: original name unknown.

X-games: extreme sports, i.e., skateboarding, one of the competitions featured in the annual X-games.

XXL: a hip-hop magazine.

ya': you.

yackety-yack: chatter.

Yacktown: Pontiac, Michigan.

ya'll: you-all.

yank his coat: 1) make aware. 2) confront. 3) a call to get someone's attention.

yappin': complaining.

yard: party. (Jamaica)

Yardie gangs: London-based street gangs. (UK)

yardies: people at an open-air parties or bashes. (Jamaica)

ya' see/ya' heard: you understand.

yawnfest: boring event.

Yay: Oakland, California.

ya-yo: cocaine.

yeasties: woman with tight-fitting pants that show the split of her vagina.

yellow bottle: Cristal champagne. A.k.a. Cris, Crissy.

yens: you all. (PA)

y'hurrme: you heard me? (DS)

Y.O.: Yonkers, New York.

yo': 1) you. 2) yes.

yola: cocaine.

you better work: words of encouragement and support for someone doing their thing.

you feel me: do you get where I'm coming from? Are we connecting?

you go girl: a statement of support to a woman doing her thing.

you need to quit: stop lying; stop whatever action is in disbelief.

young'uns: children.

youngblood: term of familiar address.

young buck: young person without skills but who makes the effort.

you not mad at me: you agree with me, don't you?

you're killin' me: you're hurting me, usually in a good way, but not literally.

you teed for that: credit for doing something.

yuck: not good.

zapped: 1) painted (graffiti). 2) tired, exhausted, or drained.

Zig-Zags: rolling paper.

'zine: magazine.

zooted: high on drugs.

zootie: marijuana mixed with crack cocaine.

z's: sleep.

To be continued . . .

english to slanguage

accept: come to grips, get a grip, bet.

account: books.

acquitted: beat the rap, teflon.

adult play room: boom boom room.

again: one-mo-gen.

agents who collect money to make sure artists get paid: ASCAP, ESAC, BMI.

agree: word/word up, (I'm) hip, ha, hello, fine, bet.

AIDS: bit, blicky.

Al Hajj Malik Al Shabazz: Malcolm X.

Alabama: bama.

alcoholic beverage: Alize, spirits, juice, Grain, Brass Monkey.

all of: alla'.

also: to boot.

always known as: a.k.a.

A.M.: the other side of midnight.

angry/mad: a-g, aggie, vexed, ticked off, sounding off, shitting bricks, ape.

annual Black college picnic in Atlanta: Freaknic.

apology: my bad.

Arabs: camel Jockeys.

argue: clown, carryin' on.

Arkansas: A-State.

art of brilliant colors and cryptic intricacy: graffiti.

Artist and Repertoire: A&R.

artist with only one good song: one-hit wonder, flash in the pan, fifteen minutes of fame.

Asians: Nips.

asleep: z's, shut eye, assed out.

assets: goods.

athletic shoes with shell toe front: shell toe Adidas. Run-D.M.C. wore and brought international attention to the shoe.

athletic shoes: tennis shoes, gym shoes, sneakers, high tops, handles.

a threat not to challenge the unknown: act like you know.

Atlanta residents: ATLiens.

Atlanta University Center: AUC—collection of Black colleges and universities.

Atlanta, GA: Hotlanta. Southwest Atlanta: SWAT, A-Town, A-T-L.

attitude: 'tude.

attractive: phat, got it going on, givin' it up, cute.

attractive tall person: tall drink of water.

avenue: ave.

average: Joe.

aware: up on it.

b <<<

bad (not good): wood, wack, ugly, stank, shit, monster, janky, ill, hit, willies, heebies, flawed, dog food, bunk, bootsy, roach, backyard boogy, bold bullshit, butt.

bad luck: the breaks, S-O-L, all hell broke loose.

bad situation/trapped: jam, jammy.

bad-smelling/stinking: sounding off, hummin', kickin', funky.

badly dressed male: Rollo.

ballad: slow jam.

basketball: ball, rock, five on five, b-ball.

bass: trunk thump.

beat in competition: slam, ripped.

Bedford-Stuyvesant, Brooklyn, NY: Bed-Stuy.

beer: wu-juice, O.E., forty, forty dog, brewski.

behave wildly: act a donkey, ape, brand-new, buck, buckwild, bug.

being true to one's African American spirit and respect for the African American culture: afro humanistic.

Belvedere (vodka): Belvi.

Berkeley, CA: B-Town.

better known as: b.k.a.

big spender/spending: livin' large, jonesing, ghetto superstar, hummer'n 'em, hollyhood, Big Willie/Big Willona, big time, baller.

bike: BMX.

birthname: government handle.

bisexual: trade (male), three, acey-deucey, switch hitter.

bitch: bee-yotch; bia, bia.

Black: nu.

Black and Hispanic: Boricua (Hispanic), Morena (Black), Blatino.

Black Entertainment Television: BET.

Black female: ghetto queen, brown sugah.

Black male: the usual suspect.

Black man who caters to, acts, or who wants to be White: Uncle Tom, oreo, house nigga.

Black person: nigger (offensive).

bluffing: write a check yo' ass can't cash, selling wolf tickets.

BMW: Beamer, BM.

bold/confident: saying, ain't no shame in my game; giving attitude.

bold: bitchin'.

boring event/person: yawnfest, square, sleeper, blasé-blah.

Boston, MA: Beantown.

bourgeois: boogee.

bourgeois and ghetto: boughetto (MO).

bowel movement: bm.

boy: bwoy.

brag: biggin' up.

bragging: talking' trash, talkin' shit/shit talkin', on swoll, enough said, name dropping, high-sidin', flossin', flexin', ego-trippin', blowin' smoke, can't hold a candle to me, ain't no shame in my game, brand-new, biggin' up, big head.

braids: plaits, cornrows.

brand of car speakers: Alpine.

break dance: air tracks, body rock.

break-dancer: b-boy, b-girl, body rockers.

breasts: t's, titties, tetas, peaches, watermelons, cannons, boobs, Big Macs.

Broadcast Data System: BDS.

Bronx, NY: Boogie/Boogie Down, BX.

Brooklyn, NY: BK, Crooklyn.

brother: blood, bruh, bro.

bullshit: fugasi, BS.

Burger King Restaurant: BK.

business: biz, caper, beeswax.

butt: trunk, rump, fannie, bump in yo trunk, baby got back, back, booty, junk in trunk.

buy: cop.

buy drink: bar-up.

Cadillac: 'Lac.

California: Cali.

call me: holla' back, hit me up, get at me.

call often: blow up.

car: whip, ride, grip, boilers.

carrying a weapon: strapped, slangin' iron, packin'.

car speakers: Alpine, woofs, bump in the trunk.

car with custom wheels that sit low: low ridas.

caught: bust.

cell phone: celly.

cemetery: bone yard.

certain/sure: shoida than sho, sho-nuff, fa'sho.

challenge/lyrical battles between MC's: underground battles, get in that ass, get up on this, eat that nigga', cut his throat, cutthroat, get at me, come hard, come correct, clash, cipher, catch bodies, battle, war.

check out a scene: drive-by, case, bust.

Chicago, IL: Chi-Town, Windy City.

children: young'uns, seeds.

Chinese people: Chinx (offensive).

chit-chat: blabber, bumpin'gums, busy lips.

choice to do or die: ride or die.

cigar dumped of its tobacco and filled with marijuana: big fatty, blunt.

cigarettes: cancer sticks.

cigars: black and mild.

clean (no cussing) lyrics: soft, nursery rhyme, radio-ready, ragamuffin music, jiggy, hygienic lyricist.

clean: ajax, beamin'.

Cleveland, OH: C-Town.

close relationship: tight.

clothes: threads, street heat, sag, get up, gear.

cocaine or cocaine use: yola, snow, ski trip, powder, key, ice cream, eight ball, dust, bricks, blow, bird.

cold weather: brick, hawk.

collaboration: collabo.

Colored People Time: CPT, means late.

come here: back dat ass up.

comedy showcase: *Def Comedy Jams.*

company: comps.

compete/take to a higher level: up the stakes, take no prisoners, step to me, send it up, serve up, run for the money, put your money where your mouth is.

complaining: yappin', cryin' the blues, choppin', blah-blah, bitchin'.

compliment: to die for, I ain't mad at cha', big ups.

Compton, CA: CPT.

concern: pressed.

condoms: skins, Magnums, jimmy hat.

connecting with someone: you feel me (rhetorical), vibe, key, feelin' it.

conscious rap: alterna-rap.

consider: marinate.

conversation: cipher.

copy: bite.

correct: on the money, on point.

cost/expensive: taxing, run.

country: bama, bumpkin.

courage: balls.

crack cocaine: woolers, smack, rock, heebies.

crave/desire: jones's, feen.

crazy: bootsy (CA), blinked.

creative language/creative language makers: slanguage, Wu-bonics, slang doctors, rapspeak.

Cristal (champagne): Crissy.

cruise: bounce, low-ride.

cry: ball.

d<<<

dance well: bug.

dance where elbows are thrown forward to the beat of music: throwing bows.

date: kick/kickin' it, hook up, dutch.

dead/dead body/die: slab, ice, give up the ghost, checked out, bagged.

deliver: bring it.

demanding/needy: high maintenance.

demonstration (of artist's work): demo.

deny: shoot down.

Detroit: The D.

dialect: patois, gumbo.

diamond: rock, seller of ten million plus of a single record or album, ice, bling bling.

diarrhea: runs.

dictionary: book of words.

did wrong: fucked.

digging in nose: diggin' for gold.

dislike: ain't feeling that, blow off.

disloyal/underhanded: turncoat, snaky, shit on, roach, fucked, flake, doin' dirt, creep, buster.

disrespect/disregard: buck the system, dis, shade.

division among a group: set trippin'.

DJ and MC: break beat DJ.

DJ battlers: wax warriors.

DJ: turntablist, spin doctor, spin master, crab scratcher, finger dancer, back spinner.

dominos: bones.

Dom Pérignon champagne: Dom P.

dreadlocks: locks.

drunk: twisted, tow down, lit, loaded, full, bent.

drug dealer: track-worker, street pharmacist, roller, jit, candy man, baller.

drug house/street with illegal activity happening: hot block, donut shop.

drugs: rocket, narc, love boat, kiss, illmatic, ice, fix, dro, dope, candy.

drugs and alcohol: DNA.

drug trafficker: mule.

drug use/user: rock star, crack feen, weed head, high, beaming, loaded, beam me up Scotty, buzzin', contact.

e <<<

East Orange, NJ: Ill-Town.

easy: keep it light.

ecstasy: e, x, love drug, ex.

ego: big head.

ejaculate: bust a nut.

embarrassed: face-cracked.

encouraging words/credit: you better work, you go girl, you go boy, you teed for that, work it, turn it out, points, go, dap, b-up.

end: ovah, done, kick to the curb, deaded, curtains, can, boot.

endowed male: packin', mandingo, hung.

endure the consequences: pay the piper, face the noise.

enter: bumrush.

equalizer: EQ.

erect penis: woody, hard.

erratic/unusual behavior: wig/wiggin' out, wildin'/wildin' out, trippin, skitzing, plucked, buggin', fruit loop, lunchin', loco, illin', head case, bananas, flipped out, crazy, act a donkey.

exact: to a tee, dead on the money.

exaggerated behavior: drama, drama's mama, constama, conflama.

excellent: a-1, all that.

excited/high energy: trunk, stoked, gassed, amped.

exciting music: tunnel-banger.

exclamation: boo-yaa, what.

exhausted: wood, whipped, tore out the frame, taxed.

exhibiting behavior that begs for attention: showing off.

expensive jewelry: bezzled out, bling-bling.

experienced person: student of life.

explain: break it down.

f<<<

face: mug, grill.

fail: bomb, tank, bricked, bomb.

failure: bug-a-boo.

fake: beat.

fake hair: wig, extensions, weave, hair dos, hair don'ts, jheri curl; dyed, fried, and layed to the side.

fashion makeup: M.A.C.

fastest rapper on earth 1992: Twista, Carl T. Mitchell.

federal government: feds.

female: tics, tank, tender, tenderoni, shorty/shawty, shero, peach, lolos, karena, hottie, hot girl, honey, gul, fem, eye candy, dime, chick, candy bar, around the way girl, bird, biscuit, bizzo, betty, beddies, bend.

female antimysogynists hip-hop collective: Anomalies.

female gang member: gangstress.

female ignorant to establishment ways: ghetto girl.

female or person who performs oral sex: chickenhead, kneepads.

female who only hangs with gay men: fag hag.

feminine lesbian: flower.

fight/punch/hit: wack, wax, thump, throw down, tag, sucker-punch, steal, stole, scrap, roll on, roll up roll/rollin', pull up, pop, mash, let's get it on, get with, knuckle up, get down, gank, clock, bust, bumrush, bodied, beef, beat down, bang, bounce.

fighters for justice: urban soldiers, soulja/soldiers.

fire/dismiss/end/unemploy: through, bounce, boot.

fire hydrant: johnny pump.

first song released from upcoming album: teaser.

flatter: jock.

flat tire: blow out.

flavored stick: chew stick.

flirt/seduce: talk to, rap, push up, hawk, clock, cat eye.

food/restaurant: eats.

for: fa.

for your information: FYI.

freestyle dance with fast movements, flip and spins: break dancing.

friend: ace-boon-koon, blood, ace-deuce.

from the neighborhood: around the way.

fun/good time: trippin', Times Square, ham it up, throwin' up the set, throw down, swerve, live, in jump, high, happy camper, groove, giggin', get your swerve on, funkdafied, dick around, cuttin' up, crunk, (acting) crazy, clownin', amped, buggin', bubblin', buck wild, wildin' out, ball up, ball out, ball.

gang boss: nino.

gang member: O-G, B-G.

gang: wrecking crew.

gangster on record but not in real life: studio gangster, thug posturing, psuedo thug.

gangster: G.

gay: sweet, sugar in tank, strawberry fruit-gazee, fag, flame, fem.

gift with purchase: GWP.

girlfriend/boyfriend: boo.

God: G, day-by-day ruler.

going to: a.

gold tooth: slug.

good girl: around the way girl.

good music/song: sound bomb, rump shaker, head bopper, pumpin', power pill, musical blue balls, jam, garlic, fat beats, eargasm, ear catching beat, cut, crowd mover, burner, bangin', aural candy.

good voice: rotors, pipes, eargasmic.

good: bale' (Cape Verde), bananas, bitchin', boomin', blazin', whip, wicked, wet, ugly, hella, tight, trump tight, thumpin', the shit, the bomb, God, sweet, phat, swangin', stankin', unfucwitable, slammin', garlic, sick, the shit, shiz-nits, ovah, out the box, out the cage, crunk, fat, on fire, off the hook, off the chain, off the heezy fageezy, off the bat, fab, off the dome, off the meat rack, off the wall, nice, nasty, beamin', monster, mashin', mad, groovin', Lucifer, krushin, kickin', it's all good, ill, illiest, cold, illegal, hot to death, hot, hittin', gravy, bonkers, stankin', bad, funky-fresh, fresh, fly, bombay, fierce, sunny, dope, def, crankin', all gravy, all that, bumpin, bomb, bangin', buttah.

good-bye: abc-ya, audi, be up/b-up.

gossip: tip, scoop, t, street buzz, skinny, mess, maxin', low down, grapevine, hype, Cronkite, buzz, busy.

government-assisted housing: PJs, New Jack City, projects—Stapleton Projects, Marcy Projects, Fifth Ward, inner city, ghetto.

government-issued cheese: ghetto-cheese.

graffiti (to write): bomb, burn, tag, bombin' the streets, art crimes, piece, flix.

graffiti artist: writer, graf kats, aerosol artists.

grave: tomb.

greeting: pound (physical), yo, play, gimme five, dap, ayo.

groomed: beat, done up.

group/gathering: set, running crew, posse, nigganet, my people, family, drop squad.

group of rowdy people: ruffians.

group sex: gang bangin', blow out.

gun: tec, piece, nina, k-tone, juice, iron, heater, heat, glock, gat, fo-fo, double-deuce, chrome, burner, blicky.

hair product for making dreadlocks: beeswax.

handmade car: Bentley.

hanging buddy: road dawg/dog.

hard worker: trooper, ball buster.

Harlem, NY: Rotten Apple.

head wear/bandana: street scarf, head gear, nu rag, lid, Kangol, do rag.

hello: ayo'.

Hennessy (cognac): Henny.

heroin: sunkiss.

high on drugs: beam me up Scotty, beaming, buzz, zooted, contact, smoked out, sessed out, lifted.

high-powered assault weapon: Uzi.

hip-hop and jazz: boom-bap.

hip-hop and reggae: kwaito (South African).

hip-hop books: *Tha Doggfather, The Vibe History of Hip-Hop, Twisted Tales in the Hip-Hop Streets of Philly, Ego Tripp's Book of Rap Lists, Hip-Hop America.*

hip-hop cartoon: *Hammerman.*

hip-hop culturist: backpacker, beat junkies.

hip-hop dance: bankhead bounce (GA), Harlem Shake (NY), bump, butterfly, throwing bows, running man, rock, ride the beat, slam, poppin', bounce, pop that pussy, pop-lockin', jit, flares, electric boogaloo, air-tracks, bump, windmills, backslide.

hip-hop designers: Triple 5 Soul, Sean John, Roc-A-Wear, Wu-wear, PNB, Phat Farm, Lugz, Karl Kani, Maurice Malone, Timberlands, Wally's, Lo, Versace, FUBU, Damani Dada, Mecca USA, Parasuco, Napp, No Limit, ENYCE, Bushi.

hip-hop dress for white suburban males: baggie pants, T-shirt, baseball cap.

hip-hop drinks: Beautiful, Blood, Cutie, Ghetto Viagra, Guerrilla Milk, Makaveli, Num Num Juice, Real Love, Thug Passion, etc.

hip-hop entrepreneurs: hip-hopreneurs.

hip-hop exhibit: *Roots, Rhymes, and Rage: The Hip-Hop Story* (Rock and Roll Hall of Fame in Cleveland, OH).

hip-hop fan: trooper, hip-hop feens, hip-hop heads, beat junkies, back packers (see **hip-hop culturists**).

hip-hop haircuts: cut—quovadis, fade, Caesar, asymetrical.

hip-hop ice cream parlor: Outrageous Flavors.

hip-hop magazines: *The Source, Vibe, XXL, Murder Dogg, Fader, Rapsheet, URB, Front, Honey, Beatdown, Mo-Cheez, Da R.U.D.E., One Nut, FELON, FEDS, Don Diva.*

hip-hop movies: flicks—*Set It Off, Slam, Style Wars, Exit Wounds, Romeo Must Die, Wild Style, Breakin', Beat Street, Belly,* etc.

hip-hop music video shows: *The Box*, VMB, MTV, *Rap City, The Bassment, 106 & Park, Cita's World.*

hip-hop musical/lyrical styles: trip-hop, rap rock, pimp hop, high-hop (see **Cornell West**), boom bap, horrorcore, mafioso, militant, political, gangsta, bling-bling, Bohemian, hardcore, alterna-rap, conscientious-social commentary, g-funk, Miami booty shake, spiritual, kwaito, jazz-rap/jazz-hop, hip-pop, hip-hop funk, etc.

hip-hop preservation society: Temple of Hip-Hop.

hip-hop purists: underground artists, subterranean purists.

hip-hop radio DJ—first: Mr. Magic.

hip-hop record companies: Sugar Hill, Tommy Boy, UMD, Untertainment, WEA, Aftermath, BMG, EMD, Cash Money, No Limit, Flava Unit, Rap-A-Lot, Sony, etc.

hip-hop tattooist: Mr. Cartoon.

hip-hop television: *Moesha*, UPN, *The Fresh Prince of Bel Air*, *Homeboys in Outer Space*, *In the House*, *Living Single*, etc.

hip-hop websites: Lehiphop.com, Kumba-kali.com, freestyling.com, hip-hophut.com, hookt.com, platform.net, peeps.com, thefader.com, ughh.com.

Hispanic person who acts white: coconut.

Holy Bible: little black book, the word, good book.

home: stomping grounds, stable, pad, in the cut, digs, cut, crib, camp.

homosexual: suspect.

hotly pursue: goose chasin', sweat, press.

Houston, TX: Space City, H-Town.

hundred-dollar bill: hun, Benjamin.

hustling/hustler: street marketing, on the block, money maker, sack chaser, gold digger.

idiot: nut.

ignorant: ig'nant, stuck on stupid.

illegal: buck the system.

impressive: whoa, vivrant, tight, the real deal, The Real McCoy.

in control/in charge: shot caller, sewed up, on lock, get a grip, ducks in a row, all over it, bossman, all over it.

in doubt/uncertain: you need to quit, nigga please, jedi mind tricks, hollywood.

include/involve: thread, plugged in, in the mix, get with the program, feature, down by law, make the cut.

independent: indie.

infatuation: puppy love.

information: 4–1–1.

information: brainfood.

Inglewood, CA: The Wood.

inhale: draw down.

inner city: streets, ghetto, sticks, woods, gutter.

insult/joke: verbal lashes, toast, tore out the frame, talk to the hand, read the palm, rag, (toss) one-liners, jone, jonesing, gash, dirty dozen, dig, darts, c-ya wouldn't wan to be ya, cap, call out.

international hip-hop organization: African Zulu Nation.

intimidate: buck.

irresponsible female: pigeon.

irresponsible men: scrubs, bug-a-boo.

is not: ain't.

jail: bing, bang, behind the wall, belly, bid.

jailed: bagged.

Jamaica: yard.

Japanese People Time: J.P.T., usually early.

jealous person: playa' hater, PHD, misanthropy, hater, baller blocker.

Jewish person: kike (offensive term).

job: gig.

journalists: pencil pushers.

keyboards: boards.

kill/murder/commit homicide: wack, rock the cradle, red rum, hittin' switches, drop, check out, bodied, bag, buck, shank.

knowledge/confidence/intelligence: stupid, steelo, sharp, science, food for thought, edutainer.

knowledge beyond years: old soul.

L.A. street gangs: Bloods, Crips.

ladies' man: superfly, supa-dupa-fly, playa'/player, pimp daddy, daddy, mack, mack daddy, killer.

Land Rover vehicle: Land.

large lips: dizzles.

latest happening: the rage, poppin', it, hot spot, hip, cool, delo, crackin', chi-chi.

laughing/to make laugh: slay, roll, kill me, crack me up/crackin' up.

lazy/lazy person: trife/trifling, sorry, skater, nigga, half steppin', getting' over.

lead rapper in a group: top-gunner, front man.

leader: HHIC, HNIC, grand puba, top-gunner, don, architects, buttas.

leave/go: be out, break camp, break out, bust, roll, raise up, jet, out/outti, audi, dip, cut, bounce, casper, break, broke, book, be-geesee.

leave alone: I ain't the one.

LeFrak, NY: Iraq.

left coast: West Coast.

left-hand turn: louie.

legitimate: legitimate.

lesbian: dyke/diesel dyke, butch

letter: kite.

Lexus: Lex'.

liar: gully.

life: the game, g, cipher

life of struggle: hard knock life.

liquor mixed with cough medicine: syrup.

location: piece, joint, bodega (see **home**).

London-based street gangs: Yardie gangs.

Long Beach City, CA: LBC.

Long Island, NY: Strong Island.

lost: blowin' in the wind.

loud: boomin', bump in trunk.

loyal friend/supporter: soldier/soulja, I got your back, bout it-bout it.

lying: talkin' trash.

lyrics: poem, licks, rhymes.

magazine: 'zine, fanzine, rap'zines.

magazine subscription: sub.

mail a letter: shoot a kite.

make illegal money clean: wash dat' paper.

make money: get paid, clock (dollars).

male-acting lesbian: butch.

male provider: sugar daddy.

male/men: vatos, rough neck, hot boy.

Manhattan, Bronx, Brooklyn, Queens, Staten Island: five boroughs of NYC.

manufacture (CDs): press.

marijuana house/place that sells marijuana: bodega.

marijuana mixed with crack cocaine: zootie, primo, wooler blunt, fifty-one.

marijuana mixed with embalming fluid: boat.

marijuana or cigarette rolling paper: Zig-Zags, E-Z Wides, skins, rollies.

marijuana or marijuana mixture: weed, turbo, trees, tical, spliff, Scooby-Doo, roach, pot, nickel bag, meth dime bag, joint, mary/mary jane, lethal, l, la, hydro, green leaves, ganja, 420, elbow, doobie, dank, chop-chop, cess, cheeba, chronic, chronic flakes, bud, boodah/buddah, bone, boat, bomb, blaze, refer, bob, bogey, blaze, backyard boogey.

marijuana rolled with cigar paper: blunt, big fatty.

Martin Luther King, Jr: MLK.

mass commercial record production: McRecords.

masturbation: jerkin' beef.

MC/emcee: master of ceremonies, mike controller, message carrier.

McDonald's Restaurant: Mickey D's.

mean: attitude or giving attitude, bitch, stone cold, ice grillin', hothead, hard, dick.

menustration: rag, PMS.

mess up/ruin: effin' up, blow.

Miami, FL: Liberty City.

microphone: mic.

military assault rifle: ak's.

milk substitute: sugar-water (water mixed with sugar).

million: mil, m's.

mind games: tricknology, politicking, politricks.

Minneapolis, MN: The Igloo.

Mississippi: The Big River, 'Sip, Crooked-letter Country.

miss out on: slept.

mix: lace.

mix of Black and Spanish: Blatino, Boricua-Morena.

mix of gorgeous and terrific: gorgerific.

mix of poetry and music: poetrusic.

mix of scary and crazy: scrazy.

mix of slang and language: slanguage.

mix of Spanish and English languages: Spanglish.

money: trap, paper, bones, skins, scratch, scrilla, sacks, flow, chips, cheese, cheddar, bank, grips, green guys, papes, mullah, loot, looch, loaded, jing, grip, flow, fetti, ends, ducats, dough, dead presidents, cream, c-notes, coins, chips, bones, cheddar, cheese, chi-ching, cabbage, cake, beans, bankroll, Benjamins, big faces, biz-zank, bricks, butter.

motherfucker: mo-fos, mf's.

music: beats, sounds.

musical measure: bar.

music made with the mouth: human beat box.

music that came after drum machines and synthesizers: new school/skool.

music that came before drum machines and synthesizers that was heavily based on live instrumentation: old school/skool.

music that complements video game: blip music.

music thieves: beat jackers.

Nashville, TN: Music City.

Nation of Islam: NOI.

neighborhood: 'hood.

nerd: corn, herb.

new: fresh, new skool.

New Jersey: New Jeru, Brick City, The Bricks.

New Orleans, LO: The Big Easy, NO, Naw'lins, Crescent City, 504.

New York City: Mecca, Ground Zero.

nice body: ripped, fine, diesel/cock diesel.

nightclubs: whips.

none: nann.

non-mainstream music: underground.

nosy: busy, busy body, dippin'.

not much happening: slow motion.

not poised: gump/gumpy.

nothing: jack, broke, zero deniro.

novice/inexperienced: young buck, whippersnapper, wet behind the ears, new whips, new jack.

no way: fugidabowdit.

NY subway: boat.

0 <<<

Oakland, CA: Oak-Town.

obsessed: sprung.

occurred/happened/happening: went down, popped off, jumped off, it's on, in full effect.

offensive action: stunt.

okay: okie-doke, fair to middlin', aiight, blasé-blah.

Oklahoma City, OK: Tornado Alley, OKC, Dusty South.

old: ole' skool, faded, back in the day, back when.

one-night stand: hit and run.

one thousand dollars: G.

online battle ground: battle board.

online hip-hop exchange: virtual cipher, key-stylin', flow-motion, fiber-optic battle, cyber mc's, battle board.

oral anal sex: tossed salad, rim job, rimming, ate out.

oral sex: went down, go down (south), shine the skin, head, blow job, ate out, busy lips.

orange juice: OJ.

organization that counts record sales: Soundscan.

organization to serve rappers: Rap Coalition.

orginators of hip-hop: architects, buttas.

Orlando, FL: Quad City.

outdated: tired, played/played out.

out of control: whipped, pussy-whipped, turned out, run amuck.

out of luck/chances: ass out.

out of money: broke, pockets on E, smelling beans.

overwhelmed: vapors, too many things, say it ain't so, shut-up, outdone, floored.

party: bashment (Jamaican), gig.

party chant: the roof is on fire, heyy-ho, are you ready to throw down.

party spot: bodega.

party started: hype man.

pass along: kick it to you.

passionate individual music creators as a collective: Soulquarians, hip-hop hippies, hip-hop gurus.

passive person: wimp, bitch, bitch ass niggas, soft, sweet, weak, pussy, powder, mark, hoe.

PCP: angel dust.

pee on: golden showers.

penis: wood, tip, pony, pipe, piece, nob, mojo, jawn, jimmy, jime, il da-da, il pa-pa, dragon, dick, bone, beef.

people/person: head/headz, peeps.

people at open-air street party: Yardies (Jamaican).

people from Atlanta: ATLiens.

people of the hip-hop culture: hip-hop heads (see **hip-hop culturists**).

people who live in inner city: urban dwellers, inner-city dwellers, hoodies, from around the way.

perfect basketball shot: all net.

perform well lyrically: wax poetic, spitfire, rock, rollin', rip, killed it, freaked it.

person being misused/abused by someone else: tool, meal ticket.

person who hangs out all the time: corner boy, hood-rat, club rat.

person who plays records at a party: Deejay/DJ.

person who spoils a good time: buster/bustah.

person with moneymaking skills: money magnet.

petty criminal: thug.

Philadelphia, PA: Iladelph.

phone book: little black book.

phone number: digits.

physically built: swoll.

Pittsburgh, PA: The Burghs.

plan: skeelo.

play a record: spin a record.

pocket change: beans.

police helicopter: ghetto bird.

police raid: shakedown.

police: cowboys, pork chops, po-po, pigs, p-o, narc, heat, 5–o, boys in blue, berry.

poor record sales: wood.

Poor White Trash: PWT.

power: mob, mafia, gangs, gangster, juice.

power of persuasion: mojo.

pregnant: smacked up, knocked up.

prepare: boot up.

pretender/pretending: wannabe, perp/perpin', profilin', jerkin' beef, frontin', dummin' up.

pretty girl: betty, biscuit, brown sugah (Black), butta pecan Rican (Puerto Rican).

prison: up north, tomb, pen, on ice, matrix, on lock, lock down, camp, can, cage, bing, bang, bagged.

prison cellblock: CB.

prisoner: bird, jailbird, locs.

prison-issued uniform: county blues.

prison term: strikes, skid-bid, bid.

prissy male: prima dog.

private/discreet: Q.T., on the low, nunya, lay low, hush-hush, down lo, deelo, D-L.

private jet: G-4.

probation officer: p-o.

problems: issues, head cracker.

produce music: beat mining.

professional: pro.

promise: word is bond, if I say it it's platinum, through thick and thin, on the strength.

promotional radio advertisements: drops.

propaganda: hype, hype man.

prostitute/promiscuous female: trick, strawberry, slizzard, skank, skeeze/skeezer, scank, pro, O, moneymaker, sack chaser, hook, hoes, floozy, bend.

pubic hair: bush.

a
b
c
d
e
f
g
h
i
j
k
l
m
n
o
>p
q
r
s
t
u
v
w
x
y
z

q <<<

Queens, New York: The Desert.

Queensboro, NY: Kuwait.

Queensbridge, NY: QB.

radio: boom box.

radio airplay: burn, spin.

raggedy car: bucket, hooptie.

rap: bust a rhyme, wordspray, spit, slang game, story with a message, rhymed lyrics over music, tales from the hood, drop track, bless the mic.

rapper: wordsmith, stunna, street poet, storyteller, scribes, poetry hustlers, poet, mouthpieces, MVP, griot, ghetto griot, flamethrower.

rapper and actor: raptor.

rapper and athlete: rap-lete.

rap without passion: whore rap.

Rastafarian: Rasta man.

receptive: open, get open.

recommend: put down.

record/recording: track, bricks, LP, joint, EP, brick, stacks.

record of the original: dub.

recording studio: lab.

record producer: track master, track workers, beat maker, beat miner.

record that's played a lot: speaker staple.

reformed pigeon: woman reformed of irresponsible ways.

relax/relaxed person: cool breeze, cool out, coolin', chill, marinate, lamp, hang, slummin', parlay, marinatin', lampin'.

released from jail: sprung.

release record for public consumption: drop track.

remote control: 'mote.

repeated verse in a song: hook.

represent: rep.

reprimand/make clear: tell off, snap, ripped, read, pull no punches, up front, pull trump card, bust balls, pull your ho' card, pump the brakes, MYOB, let have it, nunya, don't even try it, don't get beside yourself, don't go there, act like you know.

request: dibs/dibbies.

respect/recognition: shouts/shout outs, props, recognize, big ups.

rich/wealthy: paid in full.

rich from drug trading: goodfella rich, g-money.

rich with bad credit and bad spending practices: nigga-rich.

right away: with a quickness.

right-hand turn: reggie.

right here: righ chea'.

risk it all: go for broke.

rob/robbed/thieves: tax, vicked, stunt, stick up kid, stick up kings, rip/rip off, mias, jack, cop, boof, boost, beat jackers.

Rolex watch: Rolie/Roly.

Rottweiller: Rockwilder.

ruin: blow.

S<<<

Sacramento, CA: Sac-Town.

saggy pants: ate out.

salutation/good-bye: rollo, peace, one love, holla, future, c-ya, abc-ya.

sandwiches: samiches.

San Franciso, CA: Bay, Yay.

scared/afraid: skurred, shook.

schedule: book.

scout: ear to the ground/street/earth.

second album failure: sophomore jinx.

self: dolo.

sell: sling, slang, shift, roll, flip.

sell five hundred thousand copies of an album or song: gold, golden boy, golden girl.

selling fast: selling like hot cakes, blowin' up.

sell stolen merchandise: bootleg.

sell ten million copies of an album or song: diamond.

semen: nut.

serious business: squo (business).

sex/have sex: wild thang, wax, throw down, slap sessions, slay, slice it up, slammin', rock, lay pipe, pattin' pies, nookie, mo' betta, let's get it on, get busy, knockin' boots, in the cut, in the buck, hit, get down, get with you, funk workouts, dirty, nasty, cake-mixing, booty call, bone, blazin', get groove on, ball, bangin', bangin' boots, bag, around the world, bagged, beating cakes, bend, bust out.

sex drugs: sex pockets, medina, mickey, love drug—ecstasy.

sex party: blow out.

sexual disease: heebies/heeby-geebies, burn, V.D.

sexual frustration (male): blueballs.

sexual interference: cockblockin', CB.

sexually aroused/excited: wet.

sexual thoughts/aggression: pervin', on the prowl, freak.

sex with a friend's ex: sloppy seconds.

sex with a younger person: rob the cradle.

sexy: bootylicious.

share: break off.

shit: isht, ish.

shit on (literally): brown showers, BM.

shoes: kicks, handles.

shooting into occupied dwelling: drive-by.

shot/shoot: wet, spray, squeezed off, smoked out, red velvet, pop, peel a cap, bust a cap, cap, blast shots.

shower: rain closet.

silly: boo-boo the fool.

slow down: slow your road.

smelly buildup usually on uncircumsized males: cheese.

smoke: blow.

smoking marijuana: blowin' trees.

snitch: rat, tipper, droppin' dime, busta.

snob: playin' high post, Park Avenue, Miss Thang, high sidin', fou-fou/frou-frou, ciddity.

socially conscious rap/rap with a message: verbal mind food, brainfood.

sold out: blow out.

something in its entirety: the whole shebang, whole nine yards.

song on album: cut, track.

sound made from sliding needle back and forth on record: scratch music.

Southern-acting/sounding: nelly, country, hick, bumpkin, bama.

Southern region: Dirty South.

Southern-style music: bounce music, booty music, bass beat.

Southern-style rap speaks of Southern experience: third coast rap, Southern soul hip-hop.

Sport Utility Vehicle: SUV, bodies.

St. Louis, MO: Lou's.

standout: shine, radar.

start: set it off, get busy, curtains, cherry, boot up, bust.

statement of surprise: whoa.

Staten Island, NY: Shaolin/The Rock.

steal: boost, boof.

step back: bacdafucup.

store: bodega.

strange: out there.

street: slab, blacktop.

street vendors: hagglers (Jamaican).

strip club: booty club, titty bar.

strip-dance: twurk.

struggle: belly of the the beast, the breaks.

suburb: 'burbs.

successful person: the man, baller, powerhouse, platinum respect, large, got it going on, big daddy, big dawg, big time, Big Willie, Big Willona, blazin, blowin' up, boomin'.

support: 'bout it, 'bout it.

surprise: whoa, that freaked me out, snap, surprise.

sweatshirts with attached hoods: hoodies.

switch/change: flip the script.

tailgating: poppin' trunks.

take a look: peep (this).

take advantage of: pimp, feedin' (off of).

take care of: lace, hook up, hold down the fort, hold it down, hold your own, break off.

talent: skills, raw, powerhouse, mettle, glory.

talk too much: running at the mouth.

target for death: mark/marked man.

tattoo: tat.

teach: break it down, school.

teeth: slugs, grill, fronts.

teeth cover made of gold, silver, or diamonds: grill.

teeth with gold and diamonds in them: slugged up.

telephone: blower.

television: boob tube.

terms of endearment: babe, baby, boo.

terms of familiar address: cat, fam, pana, pappi, daddy, man, m'man, mack daddy, hoss, boss, homeboy, home skillet, home slice, homies, homey, homegirl, girlfriend, g-money, dun, doc, dawg/dog, cuzzen, cat, ace-boon-koon, bro/bruh, boo, blood, babe, baby, baby boy, baby girl, bwoy.

testicles: nuts, jewels.

that: dat.

the: da.

The Artist Formerly Known As Prince: TAFKA.

the artistic response to oppression: hip-hop.

the copy cat standard: Jones's.

the creator of the hip-hop sound: Kool DJ Herc.

the four elements of hip-hop: deejaying, break-dancing, emceeing, graffiti writing.

The Rock: Long Island, New York.

the unconquerable spirit of those who struggle in the ghetto: ghetto grit.

the unexpected: quiet storm.

thick amount: wad.

thick gold chains: dookey ropes.

thing/stuff: thang, jones, jont, isms, ditty.

thirty-eight caliber pistol: 38.

thought-provoking lyrics/profound statement: mental jewels, lyrical lessons, mental nuggets, science, lyrical gems, deep, science.

threat: get in that ass, cut into, get got, down for the count, don't even try it, don't get beside yourself, don't go there, check yoself before you wreck yoself, bacdafucup.

tight-fitting cap: skull cap.

Timberland shoes: Timbs.

time past: back in the day, back when.

tire rims: vogues, D's, 20's deuce o's, double deuces.

to: at.

to call someone/cat call: yo', who-dee-who.

to give money/take care of: tear off.

toilet stool: can, dump.

to like: (be) sweet (on), on (someone's tip), dig, cutt.

Too Much Information: TMI.

top-selling artist: a-level artist, diamond.

tour assistant: roadie.

transportation: rizzi, Lex', Ac', SUV, Roaster, Lamb.

treat badly: dog.

trick/fool: snow, psych/sike, play, okie-doke, joked, hoodwinked, gank, bamboozled.

trouble: all hell broke loose.

true to one's African American experience: afro-humanistic.

truth: straight up, true, straight no chaser, right on, rilla', on the real, no diggity, keep it real, fa real dough, fa true.

turntable: wheels of steel, on the one.

ugly: busted, through.

ugly girl: biscuit head.

unclear/misunderstand: over my head.

Uncle Sam: Uncle Sham.

unconditional love: love to the bone.

underground: undie, cellar.

understand: ya' heard, Y'hurrme, underdig, see, overstand, na'mean/ nawimeen, I feel you, feel me, dig.

underwear: draws.

universe/world: ball.

unkempt girl: ragamuffin.

unsophisticated behavior: street, ghetto.

unsure/run arounds: okie-doke.

up-tempo dance music: house music, perkin' music.

use of previously recorded material: sample, rewire.

vagina: trim, pussy, trap, tank, snatch, punanny, pie, O-P-P, kitty-cat, il na-na, hot spot, hole, coochie, cat, box.

various artists on a single album or tape: mixed tape.

venereal disease: burn.

verbal competition: battle, mc battle.

victorious: bested.

video game music: blip music.

walk: swag.

Washington, DC: Chocolate City, Urrea.

wear: stomp, sport, rock, freak, bust, blaze.

Wednesday: hump day—middle of the work week.

weights: iron.

well/nicely/neatly done: whipped.

well dressed, stylish: stylin', steelo, steez, sharp, rag/raggin', ghetto-chic, ghetto fabulous, g'd, flava, dipped, dapper, chamber, beat.

well-toned abdominal muscles: six-pack.

whatever: anyhoo.

what's happening: what's the dealee yo', what's popping, what's getting, what's crackin', what up doe, wassup/whassup?

when old is new again: retro, re-up.

where hip-hop began: Bronx, NY.

white cotton tank top: wife beater (shirts).

white female: snow bunny, cave woman.

white man: the man, caveman, bossman.

white person: snow, peckerwood, honkey, cracker, W.

white person who acts Black: wigger (white nigger).

wholesome girl: around the way girl.

win/claim of victory: wreck shop, trump, murder, kill, commit homicide.

window: caller ID.

wish/hope: pipe dreams.

wish for better life: ghetto fantasy.

without warning/moment's notice: on a dime, freestyle.

words and concepts into action on stage: hip-hop theatre.

work hard: bust balls.

world: ball.

wrong: twisted.

X: original name unknown.

yes: yo'.

Yonkers, New York: Y.O.

you/you-all: yo', ya, ya'll, yens.

folk in
the know

rappers. writers. poppers.
producers. deejays.

Afrika-Bambaataa
Akademics
Akinyele
Akrobatics
Amil
Analog Brothers
Andre Rison
Angie Martinez
Anomalies
Arrested Development
A Tribe Called Quest
Avant
AZ
B.AngieB.
Battle Cat
BDP
Beanie Sigel
Beastie Boys
Beatnuts
Beatum
Beenie Man
bell hooks
B.G.
Big Daddy Kane
Big L
Big Pun
Big Tigger
Big Tymers
Bilal
Biz Markie
Blackalicious
Black-eyed Peas
Black Rob
Black Sheep
Black Thought
Bone-Thugs- and
    Harmony
Bonz Malone
Bootleg

Breakinium
B-Real
Brother Lynch Hung
Brucie B
Bubba Sparxx
Busta Rhymes
Cali Agents
Camp Lo
Canibus
Capone N-Noriega
Cash Crew
Cash Money
Catashstrophe
C-Bo
Charli Baltimore
Chi Ali
Choclair
Chris Webber
Chubb Rock
Chuck Chillout
Clive Campbell
CL Smooth
C-Murder
C.O.G.
Cold Crush
Cold Crush Brothers
Common
Company Flow
Compton's Most Wanted
Coo-Coo Cal
Cowboy
Craig Mack
Cuban Link
Cuckoo Cal
Cypress Hill
D.O.C.
Da Brat
Dan Nakamura
Dana Dane

Dave Myers
D-Dot
dead prez
Dee Barnes
Defari
De La Soul
Diamond D
Diane Martell
Digable Planets
Diggin' in the-Crates
Digital Underground
Dilated Peoples
Dirty
Disk
DJ Ace
DJ Apollo
DJ Big Kap
DJ Biz Markie
DJ Chuck Chillout
DJ Clue
DJ E-Z Rock
DJ Goldfinger
DJ High Tech
DJ Hollywood
DJ Jazzy Jeff
DJ Jubilee
DJ Kahlil
DJ Kizzy Rock
DJ Kool Herc
DJ Lethal
DJ Moves
DJ Premier
DJ Q-Bert
DJ Quick
DJ Red Alert
DJ Revolution
DJ Rob Swift
DJ Roc Raider
DJ Scratch

DJ Scratch Bastard
DJ Shadow
DJ Skribbles
DJ Styles
DJ Tommy Tee
DJ Total Eclipse
DJ Twinz
D-Moet
DMX
Dolemite
Doug E. Fresh
Dr. Dre
Drag-On
Drama
Drunken Masters
D-12
Dug 1
Dungeon Family
Eastsidaz
Easy Mo Bee
Ecstasy
Eddie Murphy
Ed Rice
E-Dub
E-40
EMC's (eternal MC's)
Eminem
EPMD
Eric B.
Eric Sermon
Erykah Badu
Esham
Eve
Everlast
Fab Five Freddy
Fabolous
Fab Boys
Fat Caps
Fat Joe

Fatal
Fearless Four
Fela Kuti
Felony
Fema Kuti
.50 Cent
Fishbone
504 Boyz
Flare
Flo-pens
Flowon
Foxy Brown
Freddie Foxxx
Fresh Prince/Will Smith
Full Force
Funkmaster Flex
Funky Four +1
Futura
FX
Gangsta Boo
Gang Starr
George Clinton
Geto Boys
Gil Scott Heron
Goodie Mobb
Grandma Rap
Grand Master Caz
Grand Master Flash
Grand Wizard Theodore
Guru
Heavy D
HiTek
Hitman
Hot Boys
House of Pain
H. Rap Brown
Hurby "Luvbug" Azor
Hurricane G
Ice Cube

Ice-T
Insane Clown Posse
Jadakiss
James Poyser
Jane Blaze
Jay Dee
Jay E.
Jayo-Felony
Jay-Z
Jean-Michel Basquiat
Jennifer Lopez a.k.a. J-Lo
Jermaine Dupri
Jill Scott
Jimmy Cozier
JJ Fad
Joe Peligrino
Johnny P
J. Prince
Ja Rule
Julio G
Jungle Brothers
Junior M.A.F.I.A.
Jurassic 5
Juvenile
Katey Red
Kaygee
Keith Haring
Keith Murray
Ken Swift
Kid Capri
Kid Creole
Kid 'N Play
Killah Priest
Kobe Bryant
Kool G Rap
Kool Keith
Kool Mo Dee
Kriss-Kross
KRS-One

Kurtis Blow
Kurupt
La Chat
Lady Ace
Lady Heart
Lady Pink
Lady Saw
Lance "Un"-Rivera
Lauryn Hill
Lefteye
Likwit Crew
Lil' Bow Wow
Lil' Keke
Lil' Kim
Lil' Mo
Lil' Romeo
Lil' Wayne
Lil' Zane
Limp Bizkit
L.L. Cool J.
Look out Boyz
Love Bug
Mack 10
Mademen
Magoo
Major Figgas
Mannie Fresh
Mark Ronson
Marly Marl
Mary J. Blige
Mase
Masta Ace
MC Eiht
MC Hammer
MC Lyte
MC Shan
MC Shan
Melle-Mel
Mel-man

Memphis Bleek
Merz
Messy Marv
Miguel Pinero
Mike E. Clark
Mike Mosley
Miss Jones
Missy Elliott
Mixmaster Mike
Mobb Deep
Mo Unique
Monifah
Mono Speak
Mos Def
Mountain Brothers
Ms. Toi
Muhammad Ali
Murder, Inc.
Mya
Mystikal
Nappy Roots
Nas
Natas
Nate Dogg
Naughty-by-Nature
Nelly
Nelly Furtado
Neptunes
Nextmen
Non Phixon
Nottz
Nucleus
N.W.A.
Oli Grant
Onyx
Organized Noise
Outkast
Outlawz
P.A. (Parental Advisory)

Pastor Troy
Peanut Butter Wolf
Pete Rock
Petey Pablo
Pharoah Monch
Phase II
Planet Asia
Playa Fly
Poetic Menace
Poke & Tone
Pras
Pretty Willie
Primo
Prince
Prince Paul
Princess Superstar
Prodigy
Proof
Public Enemy
Puff Daddy
Q-Bert
QB's Finest
Q-Tip
Queen Latifah
Queen Pen
Rah Digga
Raheim
Rakim
Rappite
RasKass
R.A.W.D.A.W.G.
   Recordings
   (Righteous African
   Warriors Doing All
   With God)
Redman
Reflection Eternal
REK
Rob Base

Rock-Steady Crew
Ron G
Roots Manurva (UK)
Roxanne Shantae
Royce the 5—9
Ruff Endz
Ruff Ryders
Run-D.M.C.
Russell Simmons
Salt-N-Peppa
Sauce Money
Scarface
Schooly D
Scorpio
Sebutones
Sen Dog
Sequence (Shaquille
    O'Neal)
Shaq
Shoestring
Short-Kut
Silkk-the-Shocker
Sister Souljah
Skinny Pimp
Slave
Slick Rick
Slum Village
Snoop Dogg
Soul Assassins
Soul Sonic Force
South Park Mexican
Special Ed
Spice 1
Spinderella
Spooks
Spoonie Gee
Starsky
Stetsasonic
Stevie J

Stevie Wonder
St. Lunatics
Stone Rivers
Sugar Hill Gang
Swizz Beatz
Taki 183
Talib Kweli
Tats Cru
Tear-De-Club-Up-Thugs
Teddy Riley
Teena Marie
Terrance "Gangsta"
    Williams
Terror Squad Crew
The Beatnuts
The Cool 5
The Crazy 5
The Electric-Boogaloos
The Firm
The Force MD's
The Fugees
The Furious Five
The Gang Squad
The Get Fresh Crew
The Invisibl Skratch-
    Picklz
The Juice Crew
The Last Poets
The Lox
The Luniz
The Mysterious Poppers
The Pharcyde
The Real Roxanne
The Rock
The Roots
The Spinstas
3rd Base
Third Eye Movement
Three 6 Mafia

Ticallion Stallion
Timbaland
Tone Loc
Tony Touch
Too Short
Tracey Lee
Treacherous 3
Trick Daddy
Tricky
Trim
Trina
Triple Beam
Tupac
Turk
Twista
Twiztid
2 Live Crew
UGK
UTFO
Vanilla Ice
Voices of Theory
Warren G.
Watts Prophets
Whodini
Wreckx-N-Effect
Wu Tang Clan
Wyclef Jean
X-Con
X-ecutioners
Xzibit
Yin-Yang Twins
Young Bleed
Yo-Yo
Yukmouth
Yung Wun
Zion I

I left out something. I know I did, but I'm not sure what it is. Help me get it right. We'll fix it in the next edition. Also, I'd like to know what you think about the book. Let me hear from you. Hit me hip-hoptionary@aol.com. I'll holla back.

Help preserve the language of the culture. It's all about hip-hop, something bigger than life and bigger than where you come from, ya' heard!

Be on the lookout for Hip-hoptionary™, The Game. Coming Christmas, 2002 to a store near you!

Hip-Hoptionary™
A Registered and Trademarked symbol.

www.hip-hoptionary.com